HAWAI'I
Tropical Rum Drinks & Cuisine
by DON the BEACHCOMBER

The Ideal Breakfast

Original Recipe of Don the Beachcomber

One bunch bananas
One bottle Rum
One Parrot
The parrot is to eat the bananas

Donn Beach, a.k.a. Don the Beachcomber, almost single-handedly transformed Hawai'i's hospitality industry with his exotic style, incredible vision, and business savvy.

HAWAI'I
Tropical Rum Drinks & Cuisine
by DON the BEACHCOMBER

Arnold Bitner and Phoebe Beach
photography by Douglas Peebles

MUTUAL PUBLISHING

Library of Congress Catalog Card
Number: 2001095057

ISBN 1-56647-491-4

First Printing, October 2001
Second Printing, July 2003
Third Printing, January 2004
3 4 5 6 7 8 9

Design by Sistenda Yim
Photography by Douglas Peebles
Art Direction for drink photos by Jane Hopkins
with Sistenda Yim

Mutual Publishing, LLC
1215 Center Street, Suite 210
Honolulu, Hawai'i 96816
Ph: (808) 732-1709
Fax: (808) 734-4094
e-mail: mutual@mutualpublishing.com
www.mutualpublishing.com

Printed in Korea

Table of Contents

Original Rum
List of Prices

Here is an alphabetical list of seventy-seven original rum concoctions
created by Don the Beachcomber and copied by so many over the years.
Original prices are presented as they were available:

Barbados Punch	90¢	Montego Bay	90¢
Barbados Swizzle	90¢	Myrtle Bank Punch	90¢
Beachcomber's Daiquiri	90¢	Mystery Gardenia	90¢
Beachcomber's Gold	90¢	Navy Grog	$1.65
Beachcomber's Silver	60¢	Nelson's Blood	90¢
Beachcomber's Punch	$1.00	Never Say Die	90¢
Beachcomber's Rum Barrel	$2.00	Nui Nui	$1.60
Beachcomber's Sangaree	95¢	Panama Daiquiri	90¢
Cafe a la Queen of Tonga		Pearl Diver	$1.00
Caribbean Punch	$1.00	Penang Afrididi No. 1	$1.50
Cherry Blossom Punch		Penang Afrididi No. 2	90¢
Cleopatra	$2.00	Pineapple Surprise	
Cobra's Fang	$1.00	Pi Yi	$1.75
Coconut Rum	$1.75	Plantation Ambrosia	
Colonel Beach's Plantation Punch		Planter's Rum Punch	$1.00
Colonial Grog	90¢	Puka Punch	$1.60
Cuban Daiquiri	90¢	Q.B. Cooler	$1.50
Demerara Cocktail	90¢	Queen's Road Cocktail	85¢
Demerara Dry Float	$1.00	Rum Cow	80¢
Dr. Funk	90¢	Rum, Gum and Lime	$1.00
Don Beach	$1.00	Rum Julep	$1.00
Donga Punch	90¢	Scorpion	$2.00
Don's Own Planter's	$1.50	Shark's Tooth	$1.10
Don's Pearl	$1.00	Skull & Bones	$1.00
Don's Reserve Rum Daiquiri	$1.10	Silver Anniversary	$1.00
Don's Swizzle	$1.00	Special Reserve Daiquiri	$1.10
Fog Cutter	$1.65	Sugar Loaf Punch	80¢
General Pico	90¢	Sumatra Kula	90¢
Governor General	90¢	Sunakora	90¢
Hot Buttered Rum	90¢	151° Swizzle	$1.50
Hot Rum Grog	$1.00	Tahitian Rum Punch	$1.00
Joe's Jumbo Gold	$1.80	Test Pilot	$1.75
Kona Coffee Grog	$1.10	The Colonel's Favorite	
Mai Tai	$1.75	Three Dots and a Dash (..._V)	$1.00
Marama Rum Punch		Vicious Virgin	90¢
Martinique Cocktail	90¢	West Indian Plantation Potion	
Martinique Milk Punch	$1.00	West Indies Punch	90¢
Missionary's Downfall	90¢	Zombie	
Mona Punch	$1.75		

Preface

While researching the Beachcomber's life history, which is so full of accomplishments, I was impressed with the fact that here was a man who lived several lives all rolled into one. With friends, associates and acquaintances spanning the globe, there was nothing he couldn't have accomplished if he had wanted to. The food and beverage industry, as well as the tourism industry the world over, can give a loud ovation for his innovative ideas and foresight.

Vincent Espezito presenting Donn Beach with Territory of Hawai'i House Resolution 106—which commends him for contributing to the development of Hawai'i's tourism, 1957.

He was not only a man of action, but a teacher of the highest caliber. And, teach he did. Restaurateurs, bartenders, singers, dancers, tour company operators, and travel agents from all over the world sought out his expertise at one time or another. His list of firsts includes: The concept of a convention center in Waikīkī; the International Market Place; the catamarans off Waikīkī; a riverboat in Hong Kong and Singapore Harbors; tropical rum drinks; theme restaurants; souvenir shops in conjunction with restaurants; commercial lū'au; importation of foreign entertainers to the Hawai'i scene; merchandising carts; pearls in a shell for sale;

maile leis from the Cook Islands; an American-owned hotel in Tahiti; building of Polynesian-style long houses for use as places of business; houseboats in blue lagoons; motorized San Francisco-style cable cars for transportation of tourists; promoting the cleaning up of unsightly pollution in tourist destinations; and, he was number one in presentation of all elements involved in all of the above.

Unlike so many other outstanding and successful business people, Don the Beachcomber was a "Personality." In his day he was as well known as any big-name movie star Hollywood ever produced. Syndicated columnist Jim Bishop wrote, "Don the Beachcomber had produced himself without the aid of a manager or publicity agent. And, everything was natural. There was nothing phony about the man. Because of the stories passed along about him, many believed he was a make believe legend, but he was as real as today, and an inspiration to all."

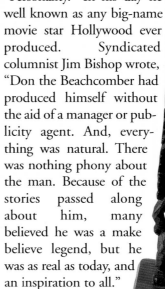

Selling a Dream

A sparkling blue horizon punctuated with graceful palm trees, languid warm afternoons on a beach of white sand—these are things that vacationers the world over dream about when they think of Hawai'i. Travel brochures will show these images, along with pictures of colorful fruit-based drinks decorated with orchids and tiny paper parasols, low-slung tables festooned with woven

Don the Beachcomber gazing out over Waikīkī beach in the early 1950s.

pandanus mats, seashells and lots of exotic flowers and pretty girls in garish pareus. The visitors will be led to believe they should wear gaudy and loose-fitting clothes and buy all sorts of useless items shaped like tiki gods, hula dancers and surfers.

There are many who will say how Hawai'i has been exploited for the sake of tourism dollars, and that Hawaiian culture has been cheapened and Hawai'i's people marginalized for its sake. But, while sitting on the terrace of a beachside hotel in Waikīkī, watching the sky turn rose with sparks of gold glinting off the water while sipping a Mai Tai—it's impossible to deny that it all works: it brings joy to many tourists the world over.

Hawai'i's international image as a tropical paradise didn't grow solely out of the Islands' natural beauty and culture, as many people think. Much of the romanticized image grew out of the dreams of a few individuals who manufactured this "tourist's Hawai'i" as we know it today. Tropical rum-based drinks, rattan furniture, even aloha shirts are ideas that came from

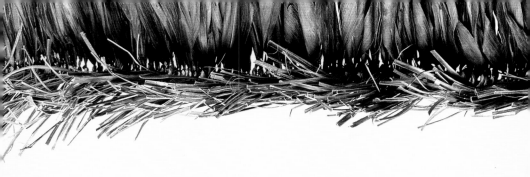

outside of Hawaiʻi, yet came to be associated with Hawaiʻi so strongly they've been adopted as part of her culture. Of those key people who created this image, Donn Beach, a.k.a. Don the Beachcomber, almost single-handedly transformed Hawaiʻi's culinary and hospitality scene. Although some may wish to criticize the contributions of a man who created the concept of Waikīkī's International Market

Don the Beachcomber resting inside his original Don the Beachcomber restaurant in Los Angeles, 1934.

Place and invented the exotic tropical-themed restaurant, there is no denying the influence he's had on Hawaiʻi's sense of style.

The Making of a Restaurateur

By the time he reached the age of 24, Donn Beach had traveled from his native Louisiana to Jamaica, Australia, Papua New Guinea, the Marquesas and Tahiti, finally arriving in Hollywood. The year was 1931, the start of the Great Depression and the depths of Prohibition. Like many others, he had to scramble to make ends meet, and he found that the easiest path to food was in the soup kitchens of Chinatown. It was here that he took advantage of the situation and supplemented his knowledge of Chinese cooking. Like other unemployed men, he found odd jobs whenever he could. At one time he found himself parking cars, another time he would be rum-running or bootlegging whiskey to make ends meet.

It was during this period of time that the Beachcomber had his dinners at Simon's Cafeteria, where he could eat for twenty-five cents. Here, he made friends with David Niven, Marlene Dietrich and Tubby Broccoli. With the connections he made in the movie industry, he soon became a

Don the Beachcomber with Oswald Henriques in Jamaica.

technical advisor on several South Seas productions, including *Moon of Manakura* and *Hell's Half Acre*. Money may have been in short supply, but Don the Beachcomber always had his dreams and his South Seas expertise, props, spears, shells and any manner of whatnots.

By December 5, 1933, Donn Beach thought he had more than a clue as to how the bar and restaurant business should be operated. On a little side street just off Hollywood Boulevard he discovered a "For Rent" sign on a tailor shop that had gone out of business. He rented this space, connected to the McCadden Hotel,

for thirty dollars a month with a five-year lease. The space was thirteen by thirty feet. As the Beachcomber had very little money, he acquired the lease by giving his word and a hand-shake. Here, he set up a bar with stools which accommodated thirty people and five small tables with chairs. He then decorated the place with his unusual collection of South Seas artifacts, some old nets and parts of ships he'd found along the San Pedro waterfront. A handcrafted driftwood sign spelling out "Don's Beachcomber" was hung out front. Two Filipino boys served the tables and two more assisted him behind the bar.

By 1934, Prohibition had been officially repealed and, recognizing that people hadn't tasted a decent drink during the previous "fourteen years of darkness," the new pub keeper started to concoct some of his most famous and unusual exotic tropical rum drinks. The first was the Sumatra Kula, which sold for twenty-five

Don the Beachcomber behind the bar of his original Don the Beachcomber restaurant in L.A., 1934.

concocted by Donn Beach. Many of them are still well known and popular the world over.

By the time Don the Beachcomber arrived in Honolulu in 1946, he was well established as the developer of the Polynesian-themed chain restaurant/nightclub. The formula of an exotic setting based on rattan tables and chairs from the Philippines, tropical rum drinks and a menu based on Chinese dishes tailored to American tastes became highly successful in Hawai'i. Donn Beach also paid a lot of attention to hiring top-quality entertainment, and some of the more famous names who performed at the Beachcomber were Alfred Apaka, Rosalei Stevens, Haunani Kahalewai and Iolani Luahine. He became well known for bringing in entertainers from Tahiti and Fiji, many of whom went on to enjoy fame in their own right.

cents. Others with tropical-sounding names were soon to follow, and were listed on the mirror behind the bar. Among these, all made with thirty-year-old rum, were the fourteen-ounce Zombie (which sold for one dollar and seventy-five cents), the original Mai Tai Swizzle, the Beachcomber's Gold, Missionary's Downfall, Cuban Daiquiri, Pearl Diver and Don's Pearl. A genuine pearl was placed into every fifth Don's Pearl. In the Zombie he used five different rums, one of which was a hundred and fifty proof. In all, more than ninety original Don the Beachcomber rum drinks were

Don the Beachcomber's DELECTABLE Thirty

COCONUT RUM
Fresh coconut milk blended with old Cuban rums and served in a green spoon coconut.
1.75

BEACHCOMBER'S PUNCH
A delicious Jamaica Rum punch of great bouquet.
1.30

KONA COFFEE GROG
Hawaiian coffee, Caribbean spices, orange honey, flaming West Indian Rums, citrus peels and Batavian stick cinnamon.
1.20

COBRA'S FANG
151 Proof Demerara Rum, Falernum and tropical fruit juices.
1.30

THREE DOTS & A DASH
• British Navy Rum, • Caribbean spices, • Falernum, —Angostura.
1.45

NAVY GROG
A robust rum punch dedicated to the gallant men of the American navy.
1.75

TAHITIAN RUM PUNCH
Exotic tropical fruits admirably blended with Mexican limes and old Cuban Rums.
1.20

SUMAKORA
Barbados and Trinidad Rums, Hawaiian pineapple juice, California oranges, Mexican limes and maple sugar.
1.50

RUM JULEP
Very old and mellow liqueur rums of great bouquet and flavor, freshened with English mint.
1.20

ZOMBIE
Created at Don the Beachcomber, Hollywood in 1934. Often imitated, but never duplicated.
1.75

DR. FUNK
Pomegranate syrup, white rums and Spanish Ojen.
1.20

PLANTERS RUM PUNCH
"One of sweet"
"Two of sour"
"Three of weak"
"Four of strong"
1.30

Q B COOLER
Dedicated to the Q Bs, gentlemen drinkers of the juice of the cane.
1.75

DON BEACH
A delightful, cold punch combining Martinique and Jamaica Rums.
1.45

TEST PILOT
Virgin Island Rums, tropical fruit juices, and our own special blend of mixes.
1.75

All standard cocktails, hiballs, fizzes, swizzles, punches, collinses and slings mixed to your order

"NEVER SAY DIE"

Old Jamaica and Demerara Rums blended with wild flower honey and Acapulco Limes.

1.30

MYSTERY GARDENIA COCKTAIL

White Rums, Mexican limes and the nectar of mystery gardenias.

1.20

MISSIONARY'S DOWNFALL

Fresh English garden mint and Pineapple crushed and frappéed with Cuban rums . . . a refreshing after-dinner drink.

1.20

PI YI

Crushed fresh Hawaiian fruits and light Cuban Rums served in a hollowed-out baby pineapple.

1.75

CUBAN DAIQUIRI

Perfection achieved through a mixture of fine Cuban Rum, Mexican limes and our own sweetening formula.

1.20

SHARK'S TOOTH

A short cocktail enhancing the mellow bouquet of eighteen year old Jamaica liqueur Rum.

1.20

MONTEGO BAY

Peruvian and Jamaica Rums, Maraschino and Acapulco limes.

1.20

SUMATRA KULA

Mellow, Old Philippine Rum, native wild berry liqueur, and juice of a lime.

1.20

COLONIAL GROG

Very Old New England Rums, Pimento Dram, Trinidad Bitters and Maple Sugar.

1.30

VICIOUS VIRGIN

Virgin Island Rums and West Indian spiced liqueurs.

1.20

BEACHCOMBER'S GOLD

Jamaica Beachcomber's Gold Rums blended with West Indian spiced liqueurs.

1.20

DEMERARA DRY FLOAT

British Guiana and Louisiana Rums blended with limes, sugar and Angostura. Demerara floated.

1.20

THE PEARL DIVER

Three West Indian Rums, our secret mixture of tropical fruit, and Falernum.

1.40

DON'S PEARL

White Rums, tropical fruit syrups, Mexican limes---every fifth drink mixed contains a beautiful genuine pearl.

1.30

QUEEN'S ROAD COCKTAIL

Trinidad Rum, green allspice liqueur, orange blossom honey, Angostura bitters and Acapulco limes.

1.10

This souvenir menu available at fifty cents

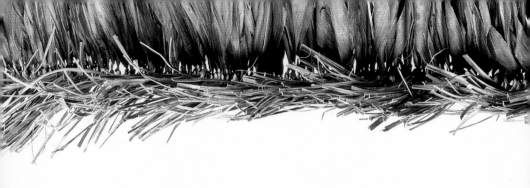

The International Market Place

No single creation in Waikīkī caused more excitement or brought more recognition in the tourist industry than the International Market Place. It was the brainchild of

Don the Beachcomber in Tahiti onboard the *Marama*.

Donn and his friend "Pete" Wimberly of Wimberly Allison Tong & Goo Architects, conceived on wrapping paper in the back of the old Moana Cottages.

The vision Donn had was to create a replica of old Hawai'i in a five-acre space in the heart of Waikīkī. The original structures displayed typical "grass shacks" lived in by ancient Hawaiians. Appropriately surrounded with coconut palms, the grounds were defined by carved "tikis" placed strategically, representing Hawaiian gods. Outrigger canoes with simulated warriors paddling them provided a feeling of vitality. Bridges with koa-wood railings were built over contrived streams and gullies to create a feeling of exploration to the different sectors of the village. Waterfalls attracted tourists with cameras.

At the very center was a grass area where Hawaiian women in native dress sat on woven mats to work on native arts and crafts for the delight and benefit of the visitors. This was a daily feature that always drew crowds for observation and picture-taking.

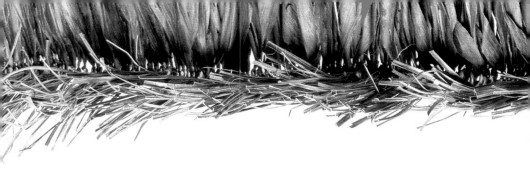

Entrance for Don the Beachcomber's restaurant in L.A., 1934.

A "grass shack" structure, part of Don the Beachcomber's restaurant in Waikīkī, 1947-1955.

Merchandise sold in the original complex was mostly arts and crafts from the Pacific and Orient. Each shop was required to submit plans to the firm of Wimberly Allison Tong & Goo, which maintained rigid standards as to shop décor and signage. Everthing was coordinated to create an atmosphere of Hawai'i and the Pacific.

An unusual feature of the Market Place was the use of treehouses. Several magnificent banyan trees were situated near the front entrance. With his vivid imagination, Donn even built a small restaurant in the limbs of

The entrance to the original Don the Beachcomber restaurant in Waikīkī, 1947-1955.

the trees, with table settings on them, covered by nipa-grass roofs. Winding stairways climbed up to the platforms where gourmet meals were served, allowing the view of activities below.

A painting of Don the Beachcomber's famous Treehouse restaurant at the International Market Place—with "service for two befitting a king and queen."

owners sought to fill every square foot of space with revenue-producing shops. New stalls were jammed into open spaces without regard to density. A new breed of shopkeeper, who spoke little or no English, took over the Market Place, selling everything from junk jewelry to slippers and clothing made overseas in Taiwan and Hong Kong. The International Market Place, as it was conceived,

The Colonel's Plantation in the International Market Place.

The International Market Place remained for many years the premier attraction in Waikīkī. As tourism grew, however, and both Donn and "Pete" Wimberly devoted their time to other projects, the standards deteriorated. The area became increasingly crowded as the

Don the Beachcomber waves from his "treehouse for two" restaurant in the International Market Place.

deteriorated and today bears no resemblance to its original concept. But the ideas and images conceived by Donn Beach live on in the restaurants, nightclubs, and other venues in present-day Hawai'i, adding the exotic flavor of tropical romance that we have come to know as paradise.

Favorites from the International Market Place Treehouse

Besides his world-famous Don the Beachcomber dinner clubs, Donn Beach also owned and operated the world-famous Treehouse with "service for two befitting a king and queen," which he built in the branches of the banyan tree overlooking the International Market Place and Waikīkī Beach. At his Colonel's Plantation Beefsteak and Coffee House, Don the Beachcomber continued as an innovator through his creation of the unique cuisine his customers enjoyed. Throughout his lifetime, whether operating his Hong Kong Lady in Hong Kong Harbor, or

Anna Gobreght, the first Tahitian dancer the Beachcomber recruited as a nightly performer.

Don the Beachcomber shares Island treats with friends.

Typical Don the Beachcomber lūʻau.

The Don the Beachcomber restaurant in Waikīkī was world-famous,
with its Polynesian-style décor and tropical rum drinks and cuisine.
It was a major part of the International Market Place, another testament to the
Beachcomber's vision, for many years.

Maestro Donn Beach, the great "orchestrator" of Waiakea Marketplace, is seen in favorite Queen's chair.

Waiakea Village Marketplace is an Exciting medley of Asia and Polynesia

SHIMMERING SILKS TO SIZZLING SAMURAI STEAKS AWAIT YOU

Isles' Most Sophisticated Shops Will Open in November

You've heard of the Thieves Market of Hong Kong and of the Robbers Den of Baghdad—and now their glamorous sophisticated counterpart: Waiakea Village Marketplace of Hilo.

This colorful grouping of Polynesian and Oriental shops, orchestrated by that world shopper extraordinaire Donn Beach, is set to open in November.

Planners forecast that the shopping experience will be richly multi-cultural: Pacific Basin plants, fabrics and shopwares . . . Polynesian dancers, aromatic South Seas spices and Island flowers . . . and foods representing every ethnic segment of Hawaii. These inter-mingle with the balmy atmosphere of Hawaii and the evidence on all sides of the genuine spirit of aloha.

World shoppers will browse among these exciting shops inspecting a myriad of merchandise which will range from exotic Oriental jewelry to hand-carved reproductions of ancient Polynesian artifacts, from original paintings and Hawaiian pink coral to arrays of exquisite bamboo-crafted objects, delicate Asian silks to a pot pourri of muumuus, aloha shirts and chopsticks.

The Marketplace is said to reflect the old truism that it takes an eccentric to find the eccentric. Much of this can be laid to Donn Beach, Hawaii entrepreneur whose eccentricities are legend. Known the world over as Don the Beachcomber, his daily attire is a safari shirt, walking shorts, knee socks, sandals and an aging lauhala planter's hat. He adopts a majestic aloofness from the madyan tree among the birds in Honolulu's famous International Marketplace, which he himself developed. Beach was chosen a year ago by Administration, Inc., the developers of Waiakea to "orchestrate" the plans for its Marketplace. He defines this orchestration as a harmonious blending of the various shops' contents and design that will result in an exciting multi-cultural visitor experience.

His expertise is the product of some 40 years as that extraordinary world shopper, restauranteur and merchandiser. The first high note in his orchestration was an assignment: Tour the Pacific Basin and return with the unique.

He returned two months later with delightfully intriguing samples of the Pacific's treasure house of the useful and the ornamental. He was loaded, too, with the kind of tall tales for which he has been famous for decades.

His bags and crates bulged with such items as lustrous pearls from Japan's Ago Bay and shimmering silks from Thailand. There was also a fascinating boar's tooth necklace from Fiji, an aromatic sandalwood fan from Mainland China and a medley of bamboo goods and jewelry from such exotic spots as Penang, Zamboanga, Macao, Ching Mai, Singapore and New Caledonia. Somewhere along the way the beachcomber picked up hippopotamus teeth, elephant tusks, trees carved of jade as well as glassincased grains of rice, each with either the Lord's Prayer or the proclamations of Mao Tse-Tung painstakingly etched upon them.

A bright stanza in the Beach orchestration has been the translation of his many remarkable food-serving ideas into reality. For instance: the Fruit of the Island pavilion. Nowhere else in Hawaii can you buy fresh pineapple juice and see it being prepared.

While he was in Singapore, he bought a minature sugar-crushing machine so visitors can sample fresh sugar juice. Hawaii's famous gourmet Kona coffee will be ground, brewed and served the customer with a Beach touch: a small slice of sugar cane as a stirrer. No plastic spoons in Beach's world!

Much of Beach's success is traceable to his appreciation that people's interest in the preparation of a unique food item nearly approximates that of their eating it. The coconut and macadamia nut illustrates this. Animation in its operation is the keynote Visitors will see how coconut milk is made, in addition to the shredding of the meat—and then sample the results.

A Rube Goldberg-type machine for cracking and roasting machine has been devised which the nuts end up between two levers, which the customer then presses and presto!—one fresh macadamia nut in hand.

The Beach-concocted Samurai Steak House, which also opens in November, merges its Japanese name with the Chinese concept of hors d'oeuvres. Parked outside will be a small cart with a variety of hot meat Shanghai cakes known in Hawaii as manapua. They can be eaten while strolling the Marketplace or enjoyed with a cup of warm sake in the Samurai Bar.

The man who answers his phone and carries on a hectic business high in that Honolulu banyan tree is now laying out plans for a mail order catalog and a sales program for the Waiakea shops. Not only the wares of the shops would be included, but also objects he buys on periodic trips through the Pacific as well as a line of jellies and jams made from Island-grown fruits.

Beach muses over this latest brainstorm. Hungry for guava jelly in Kalamazoo or need wind chimes for your verandah in St. Louis? Thumb your catalog. The Marketplace could have them to you in just hours via airmail.

Renowned for his keen sense of tropical-Asian style, Don the Beachcomber played a key role in planning and designing restaurants and resorts around the world. He was famous for his efforts at the Waiākea Village Market Place on the Big Island.

the Singapore Lady in Singapore Harbor, Don the Beach experimented with and developed an international menu of tasty food dishes and rum-based coffees. On the following pages you will find some of his personal favorites which he was able to make notes on before his death in 1989.

Rum The NECTAR of the Gods

Throughout the world, and for more than four hundred years, rum has been recognized as the one pure distilled spirit to quench the thirst, to heal the sick and to imbue strong men with the will to bold deeds.

The potency of rum for brave deeds and stout hearts has been immortalized in song and story, for where it has flowed, action has followed.

With pirates of history, Captain Kidd, Sir Henry Morgan and Captain Teach, also known as "Blackbeard"; with the heroes of the American Revolution from George Washington down to the veriest colonial volunteer; with the soldiers and sailors of both land and sea forces of America and England, rum has been the legendary drink.

Rum is a distillate made from pure cane sugar; its flavor and quality are influenced by the climate and the soil of the sugar cane-growing country; by the method of fermentation, and by the age of the distilled spirit itself.

The traditions of rum are many—mixing the perfect rum drink is, in bar room and barracks, club room and drawing room, recognized as one of the fine arts.

Included here, in the list of drinks from Hot Countries, are forty-one original rum drinks which, as served by Don the Beachcomber, are unique in that they are all of his own blending. A connoisseur of rums, and a student of the intriguing combinations that enter into the perfect drink, he prides himself on his superior talents in satisfying the most discriminating. His mastership was gained from a study of the secrets and customs of those countries where sugar cane is grown, and where rum is a national drink because of its purity, its fragrance, its nourishing qualities, and its therapeutic value.

The life-giving quality and purity of rum are testified to, even to the present day, in the fact that the Dionne quintuplets were kept alive by Dr. Dafoe through its administration. And the practiced hand, combined with the discriminating judgment, of Don the old Beachcomber, makes his rum drinks truly the "Nectar of the Gods."

Original
Rum Drinks

Original RUM
✳ Drinks

Don the Beachcomber's deep interest in the growing of sugar cane and the distilling process of rum was unique among American business-men. His dedication to providing the best rums for his restaurants led him to travel extensively. Over the years he searched the Caribbean and West Indies for the finest available. Here, he developed close friendships with Oswald Henriques of J. Wray & Nephew Ltd., and Fred Myers, owner of Myers's in Jamaica. He had such an extensive knowledge of the rum distilling process and a keen sense for the flavor nuances that several of his ideas and recommen-dations were incorporated in the manufacture of several makers' products. Several rums were specially blended under the Beachcomber's direction so that they would be adaptable and suitable for mixing with various tropical fruits.

Over time he developed the habit of making buying trips where he would purchase a two-year supply of rum for his establishments. Backed by many years of experience as a traveler and student of rums in the rum-producing islands of the West Indies such as Cuba, Puerto Rico, Jamaica, Haiti, Trinidad and Barbados, Don the Beachcomber would try rum after rum, as well as various combinations of rums, skill-fully blending them with spices and tropical fruit juices until a perfectly balanced rum drink was developed. By 1945, Don the Beachcomber was the largest single user of the beverage worldwide, serving more than 325,000 cases. Unique to his restau-rants were rum menus listing his full stock of 138 brands of rum stored in his rum cellar. These rums came from sixteen different countries. The menu also listed sixty of his original tropical rum concoctions.

The recipes that follow are the result of Donn Beach's many years of rum connoisseurship.

Many of the rums available to Don the Beachcomber in the 1930s through the 1950s are no longer manufactured. Therefore, recom-mendations are included for replacement rums within each drink recipe where necessary. Look for * Recommended rum substitutions.

Honey Cream Mix

One part sweet butter
One part honey

Heat the honey and butter separately. Do not boil. When sufficiently heated, pour honey over the sweet butter into one container. Turn off the heat. Commence whipping with a wire whip until both ingredients are well blended. Store in freezer until ready to use.

The Greatest of All Drinks

Don the Beachcomber always claimed: "Rum holds certain therapeutic values and is the purest spirit made, the greatest of all drinks because it is distilled from sugar cane, and is easily assimilated into the body's system."

Beachcomber's Gold

This delectable, mellow cocktail with its old rums, Tahitian limes, and wild honey was Marlene Dietrich's favorite. Wake up your taste buds with this tasty before-dinner potion.

1/3 ounce lime juice
3/4 ounce passion fruit juice
1/2 ounce honey
1 ounce Puerto Rican light rum*
1/2 ounce Jamaica light rum*
2 dashes Angostura bitters

Pour into blender. Add six (6) ounces cracked ice. Blend for 15 seconds. Strain into a frozen glass with ice molded into the shape of a fan.

* *Recommended rum substitutions:*

1 ounce Bacardi light rum
1/2 ounce Myers's platinum rum

Beachcomber's Gold

Marlene Dietrich

The tiny "DON'S BEACHCOMBER" bar was often filled to overflowing capacity with motion picture stars, directors and producers, all of whom had heard about the place, thanks to Neil Vanderbilt, a roving reporter from the *New York Tribune*.

Just after eleven o'clock one evening after the completion of a film, Marlene Dietrich arrived at the Beachcomber's establishment with over a dozen friends. People were already jammed around the little bar watching the original drunken Mynah Bird "Rajah" eat whiskey-soaked pieces of apple, in the end falling of his perch and stumbling while trying to walk along the bar. The Beachcomber had trained "Rajah" to say, "Give me a beer! Give me a beer! Give me a beer, stupid!"

Marlene took one of the empty stools the Beachcomber had reserved for her and her director. She watched intently while the Beachcomber began to mix what became her favorite drink, the "Beachcomber's Gold," in which he used thirty-year-old Jamaican rum. When finished, the drink was poured over shaved ice that had been tossed into a champagne glass and formed into the shape of a fan. The "Beachcomber's Gold" was simply exquisite according to Marlene. As the Beachcomber handed Marlene her favorite drink, someone bumped her and the contents of the ice-cold drink spilled down the plunging neckline of her elegant gold lamé gown.

There was no toilet in the Beachcomber's little bar. Customers had to go outside and through the hotel lobby, up a flight of stairs and down a hallway to get to one. And the restroom wasn't of proper size or a real ladies room at that. The Beachcomber quickly grabbed a towel and Marlene's arm, whisking her out of the bar and into the "Ladies Lounge." With the door open, he sat her down and handed her the towel, then turned to close the door to leave.

"For Christ's sake help me!" she said. "I can't get my gown off!"

Standing in the wide-open doorway and feeling like an idiot, the Beachcomber began to gently pull her gown off her shoulders, when she suddenly grabbed the straps from his hand and yanked it down to her waist. She looked at him and said, "Don, dry me off, quickly!"

The Beachcomber took the bar towel from her lap and started very gingerly to dry, as he told it, "each of her beautiful, pearl-shaped breasts."

When she looked up and saw his face she began to laugh, saying, "Don, you look like you've just seen a ghost."

"I have," he thought to himself. "And never a lovelier pair at that."

Planter's
Rum Punch

3/4 ounce fresh lime juice
3/4 ounce Honey Cream Mix
1-1/2 ounces fresh pineapple juice
1-1/2 ounces Jamaica Dagger Punch dark rum*
1-1/2 ounces soda water
1 dash Angostura bitters

Pour all of the above into a blender. Add eight (8) ounces cracked ice. Shake for 1/2 minute and pour contents into an appropriate glass. Serve with a straw. Add a finger of fresh pineapple and cherry on sticks or skewers.

Recommended rum substitution:

1-1/2 ounces Appleton Estate rum

Beachcomber's Daiquiri

BEACHcomber's
Daiquiri

2 ounces Cuban white rum
Juice of one large lime
1 ounce Cointreau

Place a handful of dime-size
cracked ice into a blender and shake for
15 to 20 seconds. Serve in large six (6)
ounce champagne bowl glass with ice igloo.

The Inventor

After opening his famous Don the Beachcomber restaurant in Hollywood in 1933, Donn Beach became the serious inventor of more than ninety exotic tropical rum concoctions, including the Mai Tai, originally called the Mai Tai Swizzle; the Zombie; Missionary's Downfall and the Beachcomber's Daiquiri, each drink created for a mood, climate or time of day. As an example, the Zombie and the Test Pilot were created for afternoon sipping, while the Beachcomber's Gold and Beachcomber's Daiquiri were for early evening around sundown. The Mai Tai and the Pi Yi were for later.

Beachcomber's
Rum Barrel

3/4 ounce lime juice
1/2 ounce honey
1/4 ounce Fassionola*
1 ounce orange juice
1 ounce pineapple juice
1 ounce grapefruit juice
1 ounce soda
2 ounces Ron Rican light rum**
2 ounces Myers's rum**
1 dash each Angostura bitters, Pernod,
grenadine, foam

Blend with eight(8) ounces cracked ice.
Pour into a tall glass.

*Fassionola - Fruit flavored blends used mainly by bars.
Use fruit punch as a substitution.*

** *Recommended rum substitution:*
2 ounces Myers's Original dark rum

Ambassador of Rum

Over the years the Beachcomber searched the Caribbean and West Indies for the finest rums available. On visits to Jamaica and Cuba spanning a number of years, he spent many days walking the sugar cane fields and studying the processing procedures at the distilling plants. In 1939 in Jamaica, his title of Ambassador of Rum was officially bestowed on him by leaders of the rum industry.

Beachcomber's Rum Barrel

TAHITIAN
Rum Punch

3/4 ounce fresh lime
3/4 ounce fresh lime juice
1/2 ounce fresh passion fruit juice
1/2 ounce Falernum
1/2 ounce Honey Cream Mix
3/4 ounce Jamaica light rum*
3/4 ounce Bacardi rum*
1 dash Angostura bitters

Pour above ingredients into blender and add six (6) ounces cracked ice. Shake for 15 seconds and strain into special frozen molds. Serve with straws.

Note: The special ice that is molded inside the glass must be hard frozen to retain its shape during the drinking.

* Recommended rum substitution:

1-1/2 ounces total of Bacardi light rum

ʻŌkolehau & Wāhine

In 1929, at the age of twenty-two, the young Beachcomber found himself working as the Supercargo of a relative's yacht. They were on their way to Australia, but a few stops along the way in Hawaiʻi and Tahiti were deemed necessary. After several days ashore in Honolulu it was time to set sail, but the crew didn't show up at the agreed time and place. With the help of several off-duty members of the Honolulu police force, Donn succeeded in chasing down an errant crew that had been severely watered down with ʻōkolehau, a local alcoholic concoction. It wasn't of any help that some of the local wāhine had tried to persuade them to overstay their visas. Dragging the reluctant crew back to the pier, Donn set out again on his way across the South Pacific.

Three weeks later they arrived in Tahiti several days ahead of schedule. Once again the crew disappeared as soon as their work was accomplished. And, the Beachcomber couldn't blame them. Tahiti being one of his favorite spots, Donn also left the yacht as soon as he possibly could. During his stay ashore he spent as much time as possible visiting old friends and learning more about this colorful South Seas paradise. He also hadn't forgotten about the beautiful hapa maidens, "many of whom walked the beaches almost completely in the buff." It was in the company of one of those beautiful maidens that Donn was introduced to an old Tahitian woman who called him "Marama," which means "The Far Seeing." This was a name that stayed with him forever.

Well, the very same crew problems that occurred in Honolulu repeated themselves in Tahiti. Ready to set sail, Donn quickly enlisted the assistance of the local gendarmes and the rescue of the crew was accomplished with dispatch. "It was very hard in those days to hide twenty-four light-skinned newcomers," the Beachcomber recalled years later. "But one of them did manage to avoid my rescue attempts and I've always insisted he was highjacked by some damn wahine and is still living in those lovely, lovely islands of French Polynesia with many grandchildren."

Don the Beachcomber's Plantation Punch

1-1/2 ounces Puerto Rican light rum*
1 ounce Jamaica rum*
1 ounce Demarara rum*
1/4 ounce Falernum
1/2 ounce Triple Sec
1 ounce fresh lime juice
2 ounces club soda

Twist lime peel into shaker to obtain oil. Shake well with ice. Serve in a Zombie glass. Decorate with a spear of fresh pineapple and several sprigs of mint. Locate a nice, cool, comfortable spot under a palm, sip drink slowly and let the world go by.

Recommended rum substitutions:

1-1/2 ounces Bacardi light rum
1 ounce Myers's platinum rum
1 ounce Lemon Hart (80 proof)

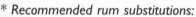

The Plantation

Donn's "Plantation" in Encino, California, was a re-creation of a South Seas paradise, completely furnished with curios he had been collecting over the years. Here, among the pandanus-covered huts and lily-filled pools, were Gala and Pagos, the Beachcomber's three- hundred-pound Galapagos Turtles. They lived at the "Plantation" and provided constant entertainment at the private lūʻau held for his many friends and the Hollywood stars who enjoyed his Polynesian lifestyle.

Don the Beachcomber's Plantation Punch

Cherry Blossom Punch

CherryBlossom
Punch

The Beachcomber describes this exotic drink as
"the haunting flavors of the Orient, and reminiscent of Cherry
Blossom Time on the high slopes of Mt. Fujiyama."

1/2 ounce lime juice
1/4 ounce grenadine
1/4 ounce Hawaiian Punch
1/4 ounce Fassionola
1-1/2 ounces Puerto Rican light rum*
2 dashes each Angostura bitters - foam

Blend in blender.

Recommended rum substitution:

1-1/2 ounces Ron Rico light rum

Presentation
is everything

At this rule-of-thumb, Donn was one of the best. The beautiful ornamental presentation, hand-held fans he designed, were in full color featuring his Chinese riverboat, *The Hong Kong Lady*, passing a wallah wallah in the middle of the harbor and announcing various daily events on board. The back of the fan featured full-color renderings of nine of the Beachcomber's most famous original tropical rum concoctions, including the Zombie, the Mai Tai, Navy Grog, Don's Pearl, Beachcomber's Gold, Mystery Daiquiri, Hong Kong Lady Rum Julep, the Pearl Diver and Cherry Blossom Punch. Each drink was flanked by a written description carefully crafted to enhance the expectations. These fans were give-aways placed on the dining tables and bars throughout.

Mystery
Gardenia

1/2 ounce lime juice
3/4 ounce honey cream mix
1-1/2 ounces light rum
1 dash Angostura bitters

Blend in blender.

Strange As It Seems

A "Strange As It Seems" article on March 17, 1938 in the *Los Angeles Daily News* featured a rendering of Don the Beachcomber with the caption, "'Don the Beachcomber' —Hollywood, Cal., café man, wears a fresh lei of gardenias or other expensive flowers *every day*, flown from Hawai'i by Clipper planes. In 4 years he has spent $7,800 for flowers. . ."

The Beachcomber would sell flower leis and other Polynesian items from an alcove just off the hallway entrance of the new Don the Beachcomber restaurant in Hollywood. This idea was a forerunner of souvenir shops in connection with some of the more famous and popular restaurants of today. At midnight every night he would present the prettiest girl with a gardenia lei.

Mystery Gardenia

Cobra's Fang

1/2 ounce lime juice
1/2 ounce Falernum
1/2 ounce orange juice
1/4 ounce Fassionola
1/2 ounce Jamaica dark rum*
1/2 ounce Lemon Hart Demerara 151
1 dash each Angostura bitters, selected
    herbs, grenadine

Blend all ingredients with crushed ice. Use a tall glass and garnish with fresh mint and a lime wheel.

Recommended rum substitution:

1/2 ounce Myers's Original dark rum

Secret Recipes

In order to preserve the secrets of his drink recipes, the Beachcomber went to extreme lengths. From the beginning he realized rivals would try to raid his establishment of employees in an effort to copy his formulae. First, he removed the labels from all bottles and used a method of codes so that employees could not memorize the various ingredients and proportions of his famous concoctions. Numbers and letters were placed on the bottles. Recipes were written in code and the bartenders followed a pattern of coded symbols indicating the ingredients, which only the Beachcomber himself was allowed to mix.

Cobra's Fang

The original Plantation Punch

COLONEL Beach's
Plantation Punch

Shake with ice. Pour into a tall Zombie glass with three (3) or four (4) cubes of ice. Decorate with a straw, stick of orange and pineapple and garden mint.

Recommended rum substitutions:

2 ounces Appleton Estate rum
1 ounce Bacardi gold rum
1/2 ounce R.L. Seale's Old
    Brigand Black Label rum

2 ounces Jamaica Planters
    Punch rum*
1 ounce Puerto Rican dark rum*
1/2 ounce Barbados rum*
2 ounces ginger beer
3/4 ounce fresh lime
    juice
2 dashes Angostura
2 dashes Pernod
2 dashes Falernum
1 ounce Curacao

The Beachcomber
Goes To War

In February 1942 the Beachcomber received a letter from Washington informing him that he was being commissioned in the U.S. Army Air Corps. He was assigned to Casablanca. On the way over, the Beachcomber's convoy was attacked by four German U-boats, and in the torpedo blast he cracked three ribs and dislocated his right shoulder. After recovery in a French hospital, he was issued a C-47, a crew, seven hundred dollars in gold and his own Colt 45. He was ordered to set up rest camps for combat-weary airmen in Capri, Nice, Cannes, Venice, the Lido and Sorento.

"The gold," Major Doolittle told him, "is just in case you get captured. It may serve to extricate you."

The Beachcomber was awarded the Bronze Star for his efforts in France and Italy, and was promoted to Lieutenant Colonel before his honorable discharge in 1946. During his tour of duty he was the Commanding Officer of nine hotels and twelve restaurants on the Isle of Capri, ten hotels and pensions in Venice and on the Isle of Lido, and all of the major hotels used by the U.S. Air Force on the French Riviera. He also warmed the hearts and stomachs of many war-weary soldiers with his famous Beachcomber martinis and rum punches.

ORIGINAL RUM DRINKS

Cuban Daiquiri

Cuban
Daiquiri

Perfection achieved through a mixture of fine
island rum and Singapore limes.

3/4 ounce fresh lime juice
I ounce Daiquiri mixture
I-1/2 ounces Bacardi light rum

Pour above ingredients into a blender. Twist
1/2 lime round and drip into blender. Add six
(6) ounces cracked ice. Shake for 15 seconds.
Strain into frozen mold, champagne bowl
glass.

Rum Collectors

Don the Beachcomber and his escape to Polynesia influenced many individuals. Not only
did they come to visit his restaurants to indulge in items to please the palate, some of them became
collectors of rum and Polynesian memorabilia from the Beachcomber's and other copycat establishments all across the country. Jack Thorpe, a very successful businessman from Grosse Pointe
Woods, Michigan, became one of the most serious collectors of rum from all over the world. Jack
would travel from one restaurant to another and knew most of the Beachcomber's employees by
first name. The Beachcomber befriended Jack several years before his death, and always looked upon
Jack with great fondness. As of this writing, Jack is eighty-four years old, and to this day he has
never opened one of his most prized possessions, a bottle of 1907, thirty-year-old Myers (V.V.O.) Rum
labeled as Fine Jamaican Rum, Bottled in Jamaica. Jack was presented this as a gift from a glass
showcase by the Myers attorney, G.A. Dunkley, who was the Director of Myers's Rum in Nassau,
Bahama. Jack was on one of his trips in search of rare rums.

Coconut
Rum

Fresh coconut milk blended with old island rum
and served in a green spoon coconut.

3/4 ounce lime juice
1-1/2 ounces coconut milk
2 ounces Puerto Rican rum*
1 ounce Honey Cream Mix

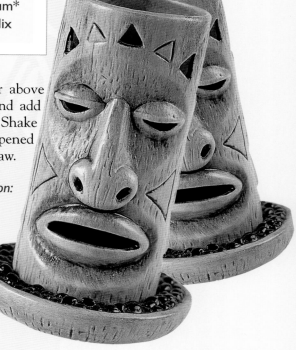

Cut top from coconut. Pour above
ingredients into a blender and add
six (6) ounces cracked ice. Shake
for 15 seconds. Strain into opened
coconut and serve with a straw.

Recommended rum substitution:

2 ounces Bacardi light rum

Clark Gable's Coconut

Don the Beachcomber was often visited in Hawai'i by celebrity friends traveling through the Islands. Clark Gable had lived next door to Donn's Encino Plantation in California, and was a long-time friend. Back in California, he had a couple of beautiful horses, and Donn loved to ride, but didn't have any horses of his own. Donn did have a swimming pool, however, and Gable didn't. They soon worked out an arrangement in which Donn could help himself to the horses, and Gable could freely use the pool. They cut a hole in the fence so they could both come and go at leisure. "Sometimes Clark would drop in and we would sit and have a rum punch," Donn recalled. "I thoroughly enjoyed the man. He was one of the greats of all time."

Not long after Clark Gable was married to Sylvia Ashley, Donn received a call from MGM requesting special housing and a personal greeting for the newlyweds upon arrival in Honolulu. Donn arranged luxurious lodging for them at the foot of Diamond Head, where he mixed up some Mai Tais and chatted for a few minutes before leaving them in their honeymoon heaven.

A few days later, MGM sent a Movietone News film crew over to film the couple, requesting that Donn set up a scenario that would look good on the silver screen. Donn responded by organizing an early morning ritual celebration in which he presented Clark and Sylvia with flower leis and special rum and hot coffee drinks in his coconut grove. Clark dug a hole and planted a coconut with a baby tree sprouting from its husk commemorating their wedding. It was perfect.

A couple of years later, Donn received another call from Clark. He was at the airport on his way to Japan, and had a few hours to visit his old friend. They met for lunch and a few Mai Tais, and talk eventually came around to the ceremonial tree. "Where is that tree? Where is that damn tree!" Clark insisted.

The two sauntered out into the coconut grove and Clark headed directly for the spot where he had planted the tree a couple of years before.

"Where's the damn tree?" he asked again. "It should be right here!"

Instead of telling the truth, Donn told him the tree had probably died. In actuality, someone had stolen it not long after Clark had planted it.

"Good," Clark responded, "because I was going to ask you for an axe to chop the damn thing down!"

Don the Beachcomber sampling his concoctions.

Don's PEARL

White rum, tropical fruit syrup and juice of Mexican limes.
Every fifth drink mixed contains a lovely, genuine pearl.

1/2 ounce lime juice
1/2 ounce fresh passion fruit juice
1 ounce fresh guava juice
1/4 ounce Honey Cream Mix
1/4 ounce club soda
2 ounces Puerto Rican light rum*

Pour above ingredients into a blender and
shake for 1/2 minute. Strain into a special
glass.

For added excitement, add one real pearl
into every fifth creation.

Recommended rum substitution:

2 ounces Bacardi light rum

Paradise

Don the Beachcomber, host to over 23 million dinner
guests at his Don the Beachcomber restaurants, often
said: "If you can't get to paradise, I'll bring it to you."

Don's Pearl

MAI THE ORIGINAL Tai

This robust-size rum drink is to be enjoyed well after the
Kona Coffee Grog and throughout the evening. With full-flavored Jamaica
rum, Don the Beachcomber guarantees that this hearty rum punch
will provide comfort, warm your blood, and restore your strength.

Into a mixer pour:
1-1/2 ounces Myers's Plantation rum*
1 ounce Cuban rum
3/4 ounce fresh lime juice
1 ounce fresh grapefruit juice
1/4 ounce Falernum
1/2 ounce Cointreau
2 dashes Angostura bitters
1 dash Pernod
Shell of squeezed lime
1 cup of cracked ice (size of a dime)

Shake for 1 minute on medium speed. Serve in a double
old-fashioned glass. Garnish with four sprigs of mint. Add
a spear of pineapple. Sip slowly through mint sprigs until
desired effect results.

Recommended rum substitutions:

1-1/2 ounces Appleton Estate
1 ounce British Navy-style rum, such as
    Pusser's or Lamb's

The Original
Mai Tai

It was at the original Don the Beachcomber restaurant in Waikīkī in the "High Talking Chief's Hut" that a very special "Original Beachcomber Rum Concoction," first served in his bar in Hollywood in 1933, was re-introduced to the public. This drink was the Mai Tai. The Mai Tai has since became so well known and popular world-wide that boats have been named after it. Restaurants, night clubs and bars have also been named Mai Tai, and, of all the exotic tropical drinks, it remains the most popular among the many millions of tourists and visitors to the Islands.

The Beachcomber's pupil, Vic Bergeron, a.k.a. Trader Vic, for years claimed to be the originator of the mixture, but Trader Vic eventually admitted that the Beachcomber had invented it. In a letter to Don Chapman of *The Honolulu Advertiser*, the well-known syndicated columnist Jim Bishop—who knew both Donn Beach and Vic Bergeron quite well—wrote the following regarding the invention of the Mai Tai:

Don the Beachcomber in his L.A. restaurant.

Part of the original garden at Don the Beachcomber's restaurant in Waikīkī, 1947-1955.

The Original Mai Tai

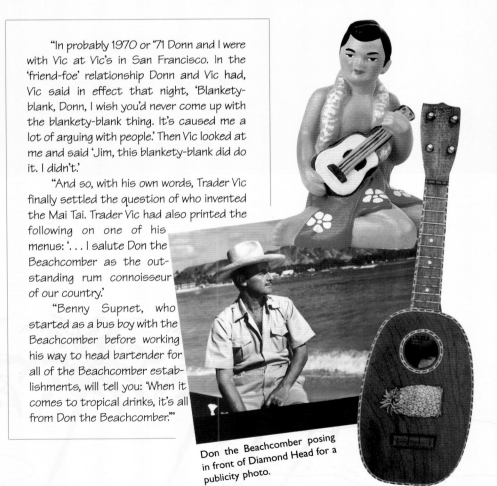

"In probably 1970 or '71 Donn and I were with Vic at Vic's in San Francisco. In the 'friend-foe' relationship Donn and Vic had, Vic said in effect that night, 'Blankety-blank, Donn, I wish you'd never come up with the blankety-blank thing. It's caused me a lot of arguing with people.' Then Vic looked at me and said 'Jim, this blankety-blank did do it. I didn't.'

"And so, with his own words, Trader Vic finally settled the question of who invented the Mai Tai. Trader Vic had also printed the following on one of his menus: '. . . I salute Don the Beachcomber as the outstanding rum connoisseur of our country.'

"Benny Supnet, who started as a bus boy with the Beachcomber before working his way to head bartender for all of the Beachcomber establishments, will tell you: 'When it comes to tropical drinks, it's all from Don the Beachcomber.'"

Don the Beachcomber posing in front of Diamond Head for a publicity photo.

Missionary's Downfall

Missionary's Downfall

A refreshing combination of Mazatlan limes, fresh pineapple, and rum, touched with the fragrance of fresh English mint. An exciting new experience, the Missionary's Downfall is to be served after dinner as a refreshing dessert and to clear the palate.

1/2 ounce lime juice
1/2 ounce honey
1/2 ounce peach liqueur
1 ounce Puerto Rican light rum*
2 ounces fresh ripe pineapple
5 leaves fresh mint
6 ounces cracked ice

Pour all ingredients into a blender, add four (4) ounces cracked ice. Blend at high speed for about 1 minute or until mixture is like snow ice. Serve in a six (6) or seven (7) ounce bowl glass. Decorate with a small sprig of mint.

Recommended rum substitution:

1 ounce Bacardi light rum

Herb Smuggling

At first, Don the Beachcomber found it impossible to locate certain fresh herbs for his recipes and drinks in Honolulu. He also discovered that certain items, including fresh mint, were banned from importation into the Territory of Hawai'i. On his way back from a Hollywood supply trip, Donn stuffed seeds and a few sprigs of mint into his hat band, proceeding unnoticed onto the plane just in time for takeoff. After clearing customs he went immediately to his Japanese gardener, presented him with the loot, and told him he would purchase all that he could grow. Soon after, fresh mint began to arrive on Donn's doorstep. After a while, he was receiving much more mint than he could possibly use. Donn suggested to the gardener that he try selling some of it to others around town. Now here was an item Donn should have kept better control of because, in his own words: "I would have made a pretty penny off of that one hat band of contraband."

MARAMA
RUMPunch

1 ounce Jamaica rum*
1 ounce Triple Sec
4 ounces 7-Up
1 ounce lime juice
3 dashes Angostura bitters
3 dashes orgeat syrup

Pour above ingredients into a blender and shake with ice. Drop fresh lime with hull into a large glass and pour in shaken ingredients. Add sprigs of mint.

Recommended rum substitution:

1 ounce Myers's platinum rum

Marama Rum Punch

The Marama

The inspiration behind his constant flow of ideas sprang from decades of shrewdly observant travel to the globe's most exotic locales. It all started with Donn's first visit to the pristine shores of Tahiti in 1929, where he fell in love with the Pacific Islands.

Almost fifty years later, the *Marama*, a daydream inspired during a visit to another of his favorite places—Aitutaki in the Cook Islands, a place he called, "the last bit of paradise on earth"—would come true. While relaxing offshore in a boat, he was struck by the obvious, that a palm-lined, white-sand beach beneath towering green mountains is best appreciated from a perspective of one hundred yards offshore in the cool mosquito-free lagoon breezes. The primeval beauty of such a landscape would be marred by conventional hotel or resort buildings. But, a floating Polynesian-style hotel room could preserve the unspoiled view while containing every amenity for the vacationer. Returning to Honolulu, Donn sat down with his friend Herb Kane, and, with rum punches close at hand and Herb, President of the Polynesian Voyaging Society, drawing sketches, the Beachcomber described his dream.

The genesis of the Beachcomber's *Marama*, was the Blue Lagoon Fa're, a Tahitian thatched hut (fa're) mounted on twin Polynesian canoe hulls. Complete with a self-contained freshwater system and an ecologically pure sanitation system, flotillas of these Fa'res would be built to be anchored in the tropical lagoons of Bora Bora and Moorea, the Sea of Cortez, the Caribbean, and in other pleasant and placid blue lagoons made just for "escape." They would be designed for a romantic and exclusive twosome, yet twenty friends could be easily entertained on the ample deck and the roomy Tahitian salon.

With a weight in excess of ten tons and a length of forty-three feet, the first Fa're was exceptionally stable. Deck space was over eight hundred square feet. Taking seven months to build, Donn decorated the interior with materials gathered from the Pacific Islands and Asia. The Fa're was luxuriously appointed with mahogany and teakwood, capiz shell walls, sea shell lighting, bamboo paneling and a woven pandanus ceiling. The kitchen and bar were fully equipped, as were the bedroom, bath and shower. An independent electrical power system was also built in. Additionally, there were dozens of those hedonistic but practical appointments that only Don the Beachcomber could imagine.

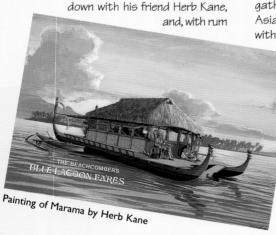

Painting of Marama by Herb Kane

Take the glass-topped dining table inside the Tahitian salon as an example. Obviously it served for dining or as a place to set a refreshing rum drink. But that was only the beginning. The same glass top afforded a view into the blue depths to watch the intriguing activities of exotic multicolored fish and other marine creatures. Powerful floodlights illuminated the waters for night viewing, and, should a lobster or an especially succulent fish come into view, the table top lifted off so that one could attempt to spear or net at will.

To complement the Fa're, the Beachcomber planned shore facilities with restaurants and shops. For those who'd rather stay on board, pareu-clad lovelies paddled alongside each morning to vend fish, fruits and flowers. The Fa're also came with a small outrigger canoe for transportation to shore.

His creation was docked at Ke'ehi Lagoon, where friends and business associates visited and enjoyed afternoon and evening rum punches like the "Marama Rum Punch." Attempting to install this revolutionary idea in Honolulu proved more than frustrating to say the least. His plans for several Fa'res along the Waikīkī shoreline as rental units for the more adventurous visitor to the Islands was set adrift by city hall.

Following the original concept, Donn Beach sat the Marama onboard the deck of the Matson Steamship *Mariposa* and took his much-admired and prized possession to Tahiti, where it was docked at a jetty alongside the bungalows of the Beachcomber Hotel in Pape'ete. When new management took over the hotel, the Beachcomber moved the *Marama* across the channel to the Blue Lagoon of Moorea. Insurance coverage proved difficult to obtain, as the French insurance companies couldn't determine if the *Marama* was a house or a boat. There was no such thing as a houseboat in Tahiti. Without insurance, the concept became infeasible, but he enjoyed living the life of a beachcomber on board the *Marama* for several years—until the dream ended when a series of three violent hurricanes hit in succession, allowing no time for repairs. In the end, the third hurricane was too much for the *Marama* to handle.

Pi Yi

PI YI

Freshly squeezed pineapple juice, blended with Puerto Rican rums and lime juice, served in a hollowed-out pineapple.

3/4 ounce lime juice
1/2 ounce Honey Cream Mix
1/2 ounce Fassionola
1 ounce passion fruit juice
3 ounces fresh pineapple juice
1 ounce Negrita rum*
1 ounce Puerto Rican dark rum*
2 dashes Angostura bitters
2 dashes Falernum

Pour above ingredients into a blender and add six (6) ounces cracked ice. Turn speed to high and blend for 1/2 minute. Pour into a hollowed-out pineapple and replace the top. Serve with a straw.

Note: Use a special pineapple cutter to hollow out pineapple. Cut a small V on the lip of the pineapple top for a straw to fit.

Recommended rum substitutions:

1 ounce Ron Rico dark rum
1 ounce Bacardi gold rum

Colonel Beach's
Plantation Ambrosia

1 bottle St. James rum*
1/2 cup golden raisins
1/2 cup prunes
4 vanilla beans
1/2 cup cherries cocktail
6 strips orange peel (zest)
3/4 cup strong instant coffee
Champagne

Pour rum into a large bottle. Soak raisins, prunes, cherries and vanilla beans in hot water. Open the vanilla beans. Add all ingredients to rum and let stand well-capped for two months.

After two months open and strain through a cheesecloth into the original St. James bottle. Add to bottle six (6) very thin orange peels—remove after two days. Make 3/4 cup strong instant coffee.

Boil three vanilla beans for 3 minutes, cool, slit open and use knife to scrape out all the little black flavor buds. Add to coffee mixture. Combine coffee mixture to rum elixir and shake.

To Serve: Fill half of a large tulip champagne glass with rum elixir. Add good, very cold champagne. Gently stir. Close eyes and sip slowly. Continue until the desired condition is apparent.

Recommended rum substitution:

St. James Spirits Royale Hawaiian Pineapple Rum

DON'S
MARTINI

I bottle Tanqueray gin or Stolichnaya vodka
I capful vermouth
Essence (zest) of lemon or lime (slice with a
    peeler to avoid any pith)

Pour a capful of vodka or gin from the top of the
bottle. Replace it with the vermouth. Add the
essence of lime or lemon. Screw the top of the bottle
back on and place in the freezer overnight.

Serving: Take an empty and cleaned 1/2-gallon milk carton and fill it with cold water and immerse the bottle in
the water. Place in the freezer for two days. Remove
from the freezer and cut the milk carton away from the
ice surrounding the bottle. Put the bottle covered in
ice back in the freezer for 30 days. When ready,
the martini will be like syrup, but exquisite.

Pineapple Surprise

1-1/4 ounces Puerto Rican Gold Label rum*
1/2 ounce Lemon Hart (151 proof)
1/4 ounce Southern Comfort
1/4 ounce Triple Sec
2 ounces fresh pineapple juice
1 teaspoon sugar
3 chunks fresh pineapple
1/2 ounce fresh lime juice

Pour above ingredients in a blender with 1 cup shaved ice. Blend to a creamy texture and pour into a scooped-out fresh pineapple and serve with straws.

* Recommended rum substitution:

1-1/4 ounces Appleton Special rum

Pineapple juice Dreams

Don the Beachcomber took over two years perfecting a pineapple juicing machine and finding a machine that would cut away the hulls to sell to farmers as pig feed. This was at a time when there was no such thing as fresh pineapple juice available in the Islands. Even the pineapple juice sold by Dole was of the canned variety.

The original plan was for a permanent open-air stand at the International Market Place that would dispense pineapple juice, sugar cane juice, macadamia nuts and fresh Kona coffee. Designs were drawn up and plans made for several pineapple stands. These round structures were called "Pineapple Trees." Being portable, the  kiosks could be placed anywhere along the sidewalk by franchised venders and easily rolled away at night. The "Pineapple Tree" carts sat just outside the lobby entrance of the Hyatt Hotel along Kalākaua Avenue. Business was brisk, but it was but a matter of days before the Board of Health swooped in and closed the operation down before it ever really got started. It seems that in Honolulu it wasn't possible to put a knife to any food sold outdoors.

Photo of the Pineapple Tree Cart.

Q.B.
COOLER

1/2 ounce lime juice
1/2 ounce orange juice
1/4 ounce Fassionola
1/4 ounce honey
1/2 ounce club soda
1/4 ounce Falernum
1/4 ounce Lemon Hart Demerara 151
1 ounce Jamaica dark rum*
1-1/2 ounces Puerto Rican dark rum*
1 dash each Angostura bitters, Pernod,
     grenadine

Blend in blender.

Recommended rum substitutions:

1 ounce Myers's Original dark rum
1-1/2 ounces Bacardi gold rum

A Chance of Rain

To increase business late at night, the Beachcomber would oftentimes go outside and turn on a garden hose which he had affixed above his bar's corrugated metal roof. This created the illusion of rain and just enough of a reason for patrons to remain for another round or two of drinks.

TEST Pilot

3/4 ounce lime juice
3/4 ounce grape juice
3/4 ounce honey
3/4 ounce Ron Rico dark rum
3/4 ounce Jamaica rum*
1 ounce Lemon Hart Demerara 151
2 dashes each Angostura bitters, grenadine

Blend in blender with six ounces cracked ice. Serve in a double old-fashioned glass.

Recommended rum substitution:

3/4 ounce Myers's
Original dark rum.

Holliday's B-26 Marauder with a replica of the Don the Beachcomber driftwood sign.

B-26 Beachcomber

In his honor, Lieutenant Ed Holliday and his crew had painted the nose of their B-26 Marauder with a replica of the Don The Beachcomber driftwood sign which had become his trademark. Along with the Pacific Ocean and a setting sun, the Beachcomber was painted sitting on the beach underneath a gently swaying palm tree. The plane and crew flew many successful missions over enemy territory. After one mission they returned with a damaged engine and one hundred forty-six holes in the plane's fuselage, but landed safely with no injuries to any of the crew.

Shark's Tooth

SHARK'S
Tooth

3/4 ounce lime juice
3/4 ounce Daiquiri mixture
1-1/2 ounces Special 15-year-old rum*

Shake with ice cubes. Strain into a chilled cocktail glass.

* Recommended rum substitution:

1-1/2 ounces Myers's Legend rum

David Niven

David Niven described the Beachcomber as he was in those days as follows: "Don the Beachcomber who was a thin, good-looking, philosophical, raffish character, was just that—a genuine beachcomber." Once when the Beachcomber was completely broke, it was David Niven who left the anonymous one hundred dollar bill in a sealed envelope in the Beachcomber's mailbox at the Garden of Allah.

WESTIndian
Plantation Potion

1 bottle Myers's Original dark rum
1/2 cup golden raisins
1/2 cup prunes
4 vanilla beans
1/2 cup bottled cherries
Orange peel
Instant coffee
Champagne

Pour rum into a large bottle. Soak raisins, prunes, cherries and vanilla beans in hot water for two hours. Open the vanilla beans. Add all to rum and let stand well-capped for two months.

Open and strain through a cheesecloth into original rum bottle.

Add six (6) very thin strips of orange peel—remove after two days. Make 3/4 cup of strong instant coffee. Boil three vanilla beans for 3 minutes. Cool, slit open, use knife to scrape out all little black flavor buds. Add to coffee mixture. Add coffee mixture to rum elixir and shake.

Fill half of a large champagne glass with rum mixture. Add good, very cold champagne to top. Gently stir. Close eyes and sip slowly. Continue until desired condition is apparent.

White Sands
Champagne Jubilee

1 teaspoon Falernum
4 ounces fine Cognac
3 ounces Triple Sec
1/2 teaspoon Angostura bitters
Thin slices lime, orange, kiwi fruit, strawberries.

Let lime, oranges, kiwi fruit and strawberries steep in above alcohol for about 1 hour.

Add four (4) to six (6) quarts champagne with ice (extremely chilled).

Add fresh mint leaves and serve.

Give Me A Beer, Stupid

Five talking mynah birds were imported from India to live in the new International Market Place and the Beachcomber taught them several refinements of the "English" language. They were placed around the overhangs of his Dagger Bar in the restaurant so that the many visitors to the Islands could stop and talk with them. "Rajah and the Hill Minors," as the Beachcomber called this group of winged predators, could speak the following: "Hello, you dumb shit! How's the bird today? Give me a beer, give me a beer, give me a beer, stupid!" They could laugh and give wolf whistles that always drew someone's attention. One bird that enjoyed the taste of rum but wouldn't drink directly from a cup was given the name "Rajah," in memory of the original "Rajah" of the McCadden Place Beachcomber Bar in Hollywood of years before. The Beachcomber would entertain his guests by feeding the new "Rajah" rum-soaked pieces of apple whereupon, just like the original "Rajah," the bird would soon wobble around before falling off his perch and wandering over on the top of the bar before passing out in a drunken stupor.

VICIOUS
Virgin

3/4 ounce fresh lime juice
1/2 ounce Cointreau
1/4 ounce Falernum
1/2 ounce Puerto Rican dark rum*
1 ounce Virgin Island St. Croix rum*

Pour into blender. Add a handful of dime-size cracked ice. Blend for 15 seconds at high speed. Serve in a thin six (6) ounce champagne glass that has been frozen in a deep freezer.

Recommended rum substitutions:

1/2 ounce Bacardi dark rum
1 ounce Cruzan Light Dry rum

The Goddess

During his tour of duty in Italy, the Beachcomber's C-47 was shot down by Fascisti soldiers. The Beachcomber escaped alone on foot and hid out in a vine-covered hole, nursing a bullet wound in his shoulder. A few days later, cold, hungry and tired, he was sitting beside a small brook washing his wound when "one of god's lovely creatures stepped from the bushes." She stopped only a few feet from him and wasn't the least embarrassed as she removed all of her clothes and stepped into the water to bathe. "She was a vision of loveliness, the raven haired beauty," he later wrote of the girl. He could do nothing more than watch as she swam and played before she finally turned in his direction and smiled at him. His shoulder healed much more quickly in the next few days with the loving care of this Italian farmer's daughter. He ate well from a hidden cache of fine wine, breads and cheeses supplied by his little Italian goddess, and, setting off for his post, he swore he would return to her as soon as the war was over.

Vicious Virgin

Pearl Diver

A happy surprise for your taste buds, this is a subtle blend of Hawaiian rums and tropical fruit syrup enhanced by the gentle tartness of Punalu'u limes.

1/2 ounce lime juice
1/2 ounce grapefruit juice
1 ounce orange juice
1/2 ounce Puerto Rican dark rum*
1/2 ounce Jamaica dark rum*
1 ounce Old St. Croix rum*
1 dash Angostura bitters

Blend all ingredients but the dark rum with crushed ice. Pour into a twelve (12) ounce glass, float the remaining rum and garnish with fresh mint and a pineapple spear.

Recommended rum substitutions:

1/2 ounce Bacardi gold rum
1/2 ounce Myers's Original dark rum
1 ounce Cruzan Light Dry
(If you can get Old St. Croix Premium Light, use that)

Pearl Carts

Donn Beach designed, built and placed the first of the famous Pearl Carts just outside the entrance of the Colonel's Plantation Beefsteak and Coffee House, where he was the first in Hawai'i to offer aged, chilled beef along with European-style coffee. Called "Deep Sea Treasures," these original "Pearl Carts" were operated successfully at great profit for several years before he sold the operation to an independent investor at additional profit. After all these years this ingenious idea is still highly successful at the International Market Place and the Royal Hawaiian Shopping Center. The concept of opening the oyster and picking out the pearl eventually found its way into many shops throughout the Islands. Today you can even find canned oysters with pearls for use as gifts and souvenirs.

Black Hole

1 good shot of vodka (90 proof)
1 good shot of gin (90 proof)
1 good shot of Drambuie
1 dash Anisette

Pour into a small glass over ice and serve.

Beachcomber's Punch

3/4 ounce lime juice
3/4 ounce Honey Cream Mix
3/4 ounce Dagger Punch Jamaica*
3/4 ounce Ron Rico dark rum
1 dash each grenadine, Angostura bitters, Pernod
3 dashes Falernum

Pour all above ingredients into a blender. Add six (6) ounces cracked ice. Shake for 15 seconds. Pour contents into a glass and add cracked ice if necessary to fill glass. Decorate with a fresh pineapple spear and cherry and fresh mint and serve.

* *Recommended rum substitution:*

3/4 ounce Appleton Estate rum

Zombie

One of Don the Beachcomber's most popular drinks, it was originally created for a special friend and is to be enjoyed during the long afternoon hours. Because of its potency, a limit of two (2) per guest was established.

3/4 ounce lime juice
1/2 ounce grapefruit juice
1/2 ounce Falernum
1/2 ounce simple syrup
1-1/4 ounces Ramirez Royal Superior - Puerto Rico*
1 ounce Lemon Hart Demerara 151
1 ounce Palau (30 years old) - Cuba*
1 ounce Myers's Planter's Punch - Jamaica*
1 ounce Treasure Cove (32 years old) - Jamaica*
2 dashes each Angostura bitters, Pernod
1 dash Absinthe, Pernod
3 dashes grenadine
3/4 ounce Maraschino liqueur

Pour above ingredients into a blender. Add a handful of small cracked ice. Blend at medium speed. Pour into a fourteen (14) ounce glass with three (3) or four (4) cubes of ice. Decorate with a spear of fresh pineapple, orange, cherry, sprig of mint. Serve with a straw. Sip with eyes half-closed.

Recommended rum substitutions:

1-1/4 ounces Captain Morgan Private stock
1 ounce Myers's Legend rum
1 ounce Appleton Estate rum
1 ounce 30-year-old Ron Zacapo Centenario rum

Zombie

Zombie

The most lethal tropical drink ever created was the original Don the Beachcomber Zombie, which was mixed as a special drink for a friend. Late one afternoon the friend came into the Beachcomber's little bar just off Hollywood Boulevard and ordered "a tall cool one" before his flight to San Francisco. The original Zombie was a real man-killer. During his early years in Jamaica the Beachcomber had learned all he could about the spirit derived from sugar cane. What all good bartenders throughout the Caribbean knew was that when several varieties of rum are mixed together the effects of each are intensified. This knowledge the Beachcomber used to his advantage. By always mixing his tropical rum concoctions with more than one variety of rum, he created his many exotic recipes. For this man-killer the Beachcomber mixed a concoction of five different rums along with other ingredients that not only looked pleasing to the eye, but were tasty and went down very smoothly.

After enjoying the first Zombie ever served anywhere in the world, the Beachcomber's friend finished two more before leaving the McCadden Street establishment. Several days later he returned to the Beachcomber's place of business wanting to know what was in the drink. It seems that on leaving the bar after the three drinks he had a fight with his chauffeur, got into an argument on the airplane, and later found himself sitting on the docks in San Francisco with his feet dangling in the water. He said that he pinched himself but felt nothing.

The Beachcomber said to him, "You were like the walking dead."

From that day on the mixture was called the Zombie and customers were limited to only two of these drinks because of their potency.

On another occasion a very well-dressed, good-looking gentleman came into the Beachcomber's domain. Sitting himself at the bar he ordered two Zombies. When he asked for a third he was told by the bartender that house rules permitted only two. Upon hearing this the man asked to see the manager.

After the Beachcomber re-explained the house rules, the man insisted, "I bet I can handle at least five of the blasted things without any problem whatsoever."

The Beachcomber suggested that since he had already had the limit that he come back another day and match the Beachcomber's one-hundred-dollar wager that he couldn't finish three.

A few days later, the neatly dressed gentleman, whom the Beachcomber had previously recognized as a member of the local mob, arrived with a couple of friends. He handed over a one-hundred-dollar bill for the bartender to hold. The Beachcomber matched the wager.

Two Zombies were placed in front of the gentleman, who in turn drank both of them down. Halfway through the third Zombie, the man's head hit the counter top.

Taking the two hundred dollars being held by the bartender, the Beachcomber warned the man's stunned companions: "Always remember the Beachcomber's Rule Number Two: Never bet on another man's game."

No one ever knew that the Beachcomber had laced the Zombies with glycerin in order to make them go down more smoothly and enter the blood system faster than usual.

Navy Grog

A robust rum punch dedicated to all gallant men
of all the navies of the world.

3/4 ounce lime juice
3/4 ounce grapefruit juice
3/4 ounce honey
3/4 ounce Ron Rico dark rum*
3/4 ounce Jamaica Dagger Punch*
3/4 ounce Navy Rum (86 proof)*
3/4 ounce soda
2 dashes Angostura bitters
1 ounce fresh guava juice
8 ounces cracked ice

Pour above ingredients into a blender and shake on high speed for
1/2 minute. Strain into a glass and add a special popsicle with straw inside.
Serve in a fourteen (14) ounce glass.

Popsicles are to be pre-made and kept on their side so as to prevent the
hole that is made during the forming of the mold from freezing over. The
hole is to be kept open to receive the large straw.

Recommended rum substitutions:

3/4 ounce Appleton Estate rum
3/4 ounce British Navy-style rum, such as Pusser's, Lamb's or Wood's

Coffee
Drinks

Tahitian Coffee

7 ounces hot coffee
1/4 ounce Cointreau
4 dashes cognac

Serve in a coffee cup with vanilla bean.

Colonel's Favorite

6 ounces hot coffee
1/4 ounce gold rum
6 dashes Tia Maria coffee liqueur
1 tablespoon whipped cream

Combine and serve in a coffee cup, topped with whipped cream.

Connoisseur's Note:

For best results, use Bacardi Gold rum.

Cafe Diable

20 small sugar cubes
10 whole cloves
2 cinnamon sticks
1 cup brandy
4 cups double strength coffee
Peel of 1 orange (removed in a spiral)
Peel of 1 lemon (removed in a spiral)

In a chafing dish, over an open flame, combine orange peel and lemon peel with sugar cubes, cloves and cinnamon sticks. Pour over brandy and ignite carefully. While brandy is burning, pour in hot coffee. Ladle into demitasse cups. Serves 6 generously.

Kona Coffee Grog

Coffee KONA Grog

A masterful blend of Kona coffee and fine rums, with a dash of this and a dash of that, Kona Coffee Grog is best served after dinner.

1 cup Kona coffee
2 teaspoons honey cream mix
1/3 teaspoon cinnamon
1-1/2 ounces dark rum
4 strips lemon peel
4 strips orange peel sticks

Into a small pan pour hot Kona coffee. Add honey. Slowly heat. Pour mixture into a coffee grog glass. In a separate heatproof pitcher combine rum(s), cinnamon and citrus peels. Take pitcher and coffee to the table. With chopsticks, remove a piece of orange peel and set afire. Plunge peel back into pitcher, setting rum mixture ablaze. Pick up flaming citrus peel and cinnamon pieces and drop into the coffee grog glass. Pour flaming rum(s) into glass and stir with chopsticks and serve.

Connoisseur's Note:

For best results, use 3/4 ounce of Ron Rico Dark and 3/4 ounce Lemon Hart Demerara 151 rums.

COFFEE DRINKS

Cafe à la Queen of Tonga

Queen Halaevalua Mata'aho, descendant to the throne of Tonga after five hundred years of royalty, was the honored guest for the two-day opening celebration festivities of the Waiākea Village Resort in Hilo, along with her daughter Princess Piloevu Tuku'aho. In the Queen's honor Don the Beachcomber concocted the following.

1/2 cup whipping cream
1/4 teaspoon instant coffee
1/2 teaspoon cocoa
1 drop almond extract
1 light dusting of cinnamon
2 teaspoons coconut syrup
8 ounces hot Kona coffee
1/2 ounce gold rum

Blend whipping cream, instant coffee, cocoa, almond extract and cinnamon until granules of coffee dissolve. Whip until stiff peaks form. Into a large cup or glass, add coconut syrup and coffee and stir until the syrup dissolves. Add rum. Top with a generous dollop of spiced whipped cream. Add Tahitian vanilla bean and gently stir.

Connoisseur's Note:

For best results, use Hana Bay Premium Gold Rum.

Cafe à la Queen of Tonga

African Safari

7 ounces hot coffee
1 tablespoon honey
1/2 ounce dark rum
1 twist lemon peel
Dust of nutmeg

Combine and serve in a coffee cup.

Connoisseur's Note:

For best results, use Myers's
Original dark rum.

Cafe Anise

1 cup espresso coffee
4 dashes Anisette
1 teaspoon sugar
1 tablespoon whipped
cream

Combine coffee, Anisette
and sugar in a cup, top
with whipped cream.

Appetizers

CHINESE Hawaiian
Barbecue Ribs

Serves: 4 • Preparation Time: 4 hours

1 section young pork loin back ribs
1 inch green ginger root
1/2 clove garlic
1/2 cup shoyu sauce
3/4 cup sugar
1/2 cup catsup
2 ounces sherry
1 tablespoon salt
1/2 teaspoon Ajinomoto

The Hong Kong Lady in Hong Kong Harbor, 1960.

Crush ginger root and garlic. Place in pan and *blend* with remaining ingredients into a sauce. Rub sauce into a section of the pork loin back ribs and marinate for 3 hours. Place a shallow pan of water under ribs to catch falling juices. Use balance of sauce for basting. Remove from oven, cut each rib and serve as a delectable appetizer.

Hong Kong Lady

In 1962 the *Hong Kong Lady*, a dream of many, many years, began to physically take shape. At a cost of more than four million Hong Kong dollars, it would be a one hundred and fifty-foot Maharajah's version of a Mississippi riverboat. Hong Kong's Governor Black enthusiastically agreed that the *Hong Kong Lady*, once in service as a unique and luxurious double-deck floating restaurant and casino, would add great flavor to an already bustling Hong Kong Harbor. The riverboat featured both public and private dining rooms, bars and lounges and a coffee house. On the top deck there was a formal dining room and dance floor with a sliding roof. Guests could cruise the harbor at night, dancing beneath the stars. More than two hundred and fifty guests could be accommodated aboard the boat. Menus embraced foods from many lands: Chinese pheasants, choice steaks from Omaha, baked potatoes from Idaho, salad greens from Hawai'i, fresh-caught Hong Kong seafood, curries from India and Burma, and some of the dishes from Don the Beachcomber's Polynesian and Japanese menus.

Green Soy
BEAN Pupus

Serves: 4 • Preparation Time: 30 minutes
Complementary Dishes: Ideal alone

2 pounds green soy beans (in pod)
I clove garlic – crushed
I tablespoon sugar
1/4 teaspoon Ajinomoto
1/4 cup red Hawaiian rock salt
1/4 teaspoon white pepper
2 bay leaves
1/4 teaspoon crushed red pepper
2 tablespoons olive oil

To 3 quarts of boiling water (medium-boil) add two (2) pounds of green soy beans (in pod). Boil for 20 minutes, then add all spices and seasonings. Continue boiling until beans are tender. Medium-boil another 40 minutes. Drain and serve hot. Pop whole pod into mouth and squish out beans.

While traveling in the South Pacific, Don the Beachcomber discovered these thatched huts set high among the branches—they became the inspiration for his famous Treehouse restaurant at the International Market Place.

Tahitian
Shrimps

Serves: 4

24 medium-size, unpeeled, raw shrimp
1 ounce dry sherry
1 ounce dry vermouth
1/4 teaspoon ajinomoto
1/4 teaspoon white pepper
1 clove garlic, dime-size—crushed
4 tablespoons fruity olive oil
1/2 cup Hawaiian red rock salt, or
    substitute coarse sea salt
Juice of large Mexican or Tahitian lime

In a cup, combine all ingredients except shrimp, rock salt and olive oil. Pour olive oil into a heavy skillet and heat until it begins to smoke. Quickly place shrimps in the skillet in one layer. Cook for 1-1/2 minutes on one side, then turn and cook for 1-1/2 minutes on the other side. Reduce heat to medium and slowly shuffle skillet back and forth over flame, at the same time pouring contents of cup over shrimps. Immediately clamp lid tightly on skillet and continue shuffling pan over the burner for 1 minute. Remove lid and sprinkle rock salt over shrimps, all the while continuing to shuffle skillet, and cook for 1 minute longer, no more. Turn out contents onto heated platter.

Have guests peel their own shrimps and season them with wedges of lime. Present each guest with a warm, moist towel when they have finished.

Note: Success with the recipe depends upon the speed of cooking. The cooking should take no longer than 5 minutes from start to finish.

Poisson Cru

Serves: 4 • Preparation Time: 3 hours
Complementary Dishes: Salad, French baguette

2 pounds fresh mahimahi or 'ahi
8 ripe limes – lemons will not do!
2 cups freshly made coconut cream, or one
　　14-ounce can coconut cream
1 large, ripe tomato
1 medium carrot – grated
1 medium-size Maui onion – finely
　　chopped
1 tablespoon sea salt
1/8 teaspoon white salt
3 shallots with tops – finely chopped
1/2 cup thinly sliced long, narrow
　　strips cucumber
1/2 cup chopped parsley
2 hard boiled eggs (sliced)

Cut the fresh mahimahi or 'ahi into evenly sliced pieces, about 1/2 inch x 1 inch. Place the fish in a large glass bowl. Add salt and stir. Allow fish to rest in the salt for 30 minutes. By hand, squeeze fish and remove approximately half the liquid. Add juice of 8 limes to fish and marinate for 1 hour. If too much liquid remains, remove half. Stir and add fresh coconut cream and gently mix into the fish. Let marinate for 1 hour in refrigerator until very cold. Do not freeze! Add carrot, cucumber, onions, shallots and tomato. Serve on three (3) large, chilled romaine lettuce leaves. Garnish with sliced boiled eggs and parsley.

Salads & Dressings

Frank Morgan's costume wowed the four on mat—Evie, Producer S. P. Eagle, Evie's John Huston and Georgia Carroll.

Connie Moore kept time with musicians on gourd. She's flanked by scarfed hubby John Maschio and Mrs. Preston.

...ce Faye feasted on Cantonese pig and ...ck. Looks like Phil made a quick ...itcheroo to Joe Collegiate clothes.

Obvious observers — Starlet Rhonda Fleming and Bandman Kay Kyser captivated by the tom-tom of the gourd.

Photos from a *Life* magazine article about Don the Beachcomber in the 1960s.

BeanSprout Salad

Serves: 2 • Preparation Time: 30 minutes
Complementary Dishes: Steamed rice, Pickled ginger

1 teaspoon olive oil
2 tablespoons lean ground veal
1/2 cup chopped green onions
1/2 cup thinly chopped green peppers
1/2 cup thinly sliced Maui onions
4 cups bean sprouts
1 large sliver young green ginger –
   finely chopped
1/2 cup chicken stock
1/3 teaspoon sugar
1 teaspoon tamari
Salt and pepper
2 dashes Mrs. Dash Hot Pepper
6 drops sesame oil

In a pan, put olive oil. Add ground veal and cook until brown. Add chopped green onions, chopped green pepper, Maui onions, bean sprouts and ginger. Cook for 3 minutes on high. Thicken with a little cornstarch.

Chilled
CAULIFLOWER Salad

Serves: 4 • Preparation Time: 3 hours
Complementary Dishes: Cold cuts, Fresh sourdough bread

2 tablespoons chopped green onions
1 cup celery hearts – chopped small
3 cups cauliflower flowerettes
3/4 cup cashew nuts – chopped large
3 tablespoons mayonnaise – heaped
1 tablespoon curry powder (scant)
1/16 teaspoon white pepper
1/8 teaspoon Ajinomoto

Chill hard before serving
on a lettuce leaf.

Crispy
Chicken Salad

Serves: 4

2 large romaine lettuce heads
4 stalks celery
2 tablespoons sesame seeds
12 strips fried wonton skins, 3/4-inch wide
2 tablespoons toasted, slivered almonds
2 cups cooked chicken, shredded into large pieces

In a glass salad bowl, break lettuce into bite-size pieces. Cross-cut celery into half-inch pieces and add to bowl. Toss in almonds and chicken.

Dressing:
4 tablespoons rice vinegar
2 tablespoons Chinese rice wine
Salt and pepper to taste

Combine dressing ingredients and toss into salad. Garnish with sesame seeds and wonton strips.

PAPAYA SEED
Dressing

Serving size: About 1 cup of dressing

1/4 cup tarragon or white-wine vinegar
1/4 cup granulated sugar
1/2 cup vegetable oil
1 tablespoon lemon juice
1/2 teaspoon dry mustard
1/2 small onion, peeled and minced
1/2 teaspoon salt
1-1/2 teaspoons papaya seeds

Place all ingredients except papaya seeds in a blender or food processor and blend for 2 minutes. Add the papaya seeds and continue to blend until they are the consistency of coarsely ground black pepper.

Chill the dressing for 1 hour and use over a salad of tossed mixed greens or fresh fruit. Makes approximately 1 cup.

Salad Supreme

Serves: 4 • Complementary Dishes: Best eaten prior to fish dinner, French baguette

Endive
16 segments ripe Pamplemousse
(pomelo or grapefruit) – cut in half
4 halves medium-ripe large avocado – peeled
8 segments peeled tomato
8 thin slices cucumber

Dressing:
3 ounce Good Seasons Italian Dressing
1 tablespoon mayonnaise
1 lime
1/2 teaspoon freshly ground pepper
1/2 teaspoon salt
1 teaspoon sugar – preferably brown
1 teaspoon catsup
1/8 teaspoon Ajinomoto
2 heavy dashes Maggi Arome
1/8 teaspoon onion powder
1/8 teaspoon fine herbs
1 ounce olive oil
2 green onions – smashed and chopped
1/2 teaspoon grated green pepper

Combine dressing ingredients in a bowl and mix thoroughly and chill before serving.

To Serve: Place half-peeled avocado on several leaves of Belgium endive. Fill avocado with segments of Pamplemousse and pour 1/4 of the dressing over each portion. Add tomatoes and cucumbers.

Please Note: Be sure all ingredients are thoroughly chilled before serving.

Meats

Don the Beachcomber perched among the branches in his
International Market Place Treehouse, "the world's most exclusive restaurant."

Tonkatsu Supper

Serves: 4 • Preparation Time: 45 minutes
Complementary Dishes: Rice, Namasu shredded cabbage and carrot

4 thinly sliced boneless pork chops
Tonkatsu sauce
Salt
Pepper
2 Tablespoons flour
1 egg
Japanese breadcrumbs (panko)
Salad oil for frying
1-1/2 cups shredded cabbage
1 cup shredded carrots

Pound pork pieces between sheets of wax paper until 1/8-inch thick. Sprinkle each cutlet lightly with salt and pepper. Dust cutlets with all-purpose flour, shaking off excess.

In a shallow bowl, lightly beat and blend one egg with one (1) tablespoon water. Spread about 1 cup panko on a plate. Dip each cutlet in egg, draw briefly, then press into crumbs to coat thickly. Set aside for about 10 minutes to dry.

In a small bowl, mix 1-1/2 cups finely shredded cabbage with 1 cup shredded carrots. Set aside.

Pour salad oil 1/8-inch deep in an 8-inch frying pan. Heat to 360 degrees. Fry one (1) or two (2) pork pieces at a time, turning until evenly browned, about 3 to 5 minutes. Drain on paper towels. Serve with a mound of cabbage mixture and Tonkatsu sauce on each plate.

MEATS

Steak
Genghis Khan
for Four

Serves: 4 • Preparation Time: 6 hours
Complementary Dishes: Steamed rice, Vegetable Orientale

4 pounds choice, chilled New York sirloin steak (well-trimmed
   to about an 8-inch width—have butcher remove excess fat)
1/2 teaspoon coarse black pepper
1 teaspoon salt
1 heaping tablespoon powdered coffee
1 piece Roquefort cheese (the size of a large hen egg)
1/2 cup prime olive oil
1 tablespoon shoyu
1 teaspoon Lea and Perrins Worcestershire Sauce
1 large clove garlic – crushed

Put all ingredients except steak into a large mixing bowl. Use hands to soften cheese and make a thick, pasty marinade. Place steak in a flat pan. Pour contents of mixing bowl over steak, using hands to rub marinade into steak. Allow to sit at room temperature for 3 hours.

Forty-five (45) minutes before guests are ready for dinner, put meat on a charcoal grill. Be sure that the coals are well spread and very hot, and keep grill at least four (4) inches from charcoal. If fat drops into the charcoal, spray water lightly over coals to prevent flaming. Cook 15 minutes on each side.

Use balance of marinade to brush on while grilling.

After about 35 to 45 minutes remove and bring to table on a steak board and slice across the grain using a very sharp roast beef knife. Serve several thin slices for each portion.

Notes: By using this large 4-pound piece of choice sirloin and broiling it in this manner, you obtain a masterpiece of savory perfection with colors ranging from charred-brown to a surprise-pink and blood-red.

Seafood

Crab Fu Yong à la Donn

Serves: 4 • Preparation Time: 45 minutes
Complementary Dishes: Rice, Salad

Requires 1 to 4 eight-inch skillet(s) to cook either simultaneously or one at a time.

Break 6 large eggs into a mixing bowl
(gently stir), add:
1 cup bean sprouts, washed, drained and cut
into 1-inch strips
1/2 cup canned, sliced mushrooms
1/2 cup celery heart, slivered at an angle
3/4 cup crabmeat
1/4 cup sliced green peppers
1/4 cup chopped green onions
1/2 teaspoon salt
1/4 teaspoon Ajinomoto
1 tablespoon dry sherry or rice
wine
1/4 teaspoon white pepper
4 tablespoons olive oil

Fold and gently mix all ingredients together.

Method for Making Individual Patties:
Into each skillet, put one (1) tablespoon of olive oil and heat. Divide above mixture into four (4) portions using measuring cup. Add portions to hot oil and cook until brown. (About 3 minutes). Turn over and repeat. With a wide spatula, move patties to paper towel-covered wire rack and drain off any excess oil.

Sauce for
Crab Fu Yong
à la Donn

2 cups chicken broth
1 tablespoon shoyu
1/4 teaspoon salt
1 tablespoon catsup
3-1/2 tablespoons flour

Heat chicken broth, shoyu, salt, and catsup, bring to boil. Turn heat down. Thicken with flour in a small amount of cold water. Add and stir slowly so as not to create lumps. Cook for 3 minutes. Strain if lumpy. Keep warm until omelette patties are ready. Serve over Crab Fu Yong and rice.

The Beachcomber In Lahaina

Donn Beach was moving to Lahaina, Maui. One afternoon he received a call from a Hollywood producer friend inquiring about a location that would be a stand-in for Papeete for an upcoming television series based on the stories written by Jack London. There also had to be a hotel close by. Well, Donn Beach knew the exact location: Lahaina, Maui. Taking leave of Honolulu he arranged the securing of a fifty-year lease on the old Pioneer Inn. The sixteen-room Pioneer Inn had been built on the island of Lāna'i, cut in half and floated to Maui. This was where he welcomed James Michener, who enjoyed a wonderful stay under the Beachcomber's roof in room six, Queen Lili'uokalani's haunt, while living and receiving inspiration for his novel, Hawai'i. Room six was where the Queen enjoyed having her subjects visit her on her royal visits to the island.

On a cold, wind-chilled day in mid-January, the producer friend with crew arrived aboard a brigantine and tied up in front of the old hotel. Here in Lahaina, three films were eventually made.

The efforts of the Beachcomber in Lahaina cannot be minimized. Here, he was instrumental in getting the county of Maui to provide the proper safeguards for the restoration and retention of the flavor and old architecture of the entire town of Lahaina. Enlisting the assistance of "Pete" Wimberly, he finally obtained the necessary funds for plans for the historical restoration of this famous whaling town through continuous lobbying efforts of the Legislature. In 1962 the county of Maui enacted ordinance number 321 providing for the establishment of the Lahaina historical district.

Don the Beachcomber's Rule Number One: "Enjoy life and spend every penny I make."

DON'S BROILED
Salmon Dinner

Serves: 4 • Preparation Time: 30 minutes
Complementary Dishes: Salad, Mashed potatoes

1 teaspoon melted margarine
3 to 4 sprinkles Mrs. Dash
1/2 pinch chili powder
2 green onions
4 tablespoons grated cucumber
4 tablespoons plain yogurt
Pepper

Don the Beachcomber, Alice Faye and Robert Preston sing a tune during one of his grand lū'au.

Charcoal broil salmon steaks and remove. In a pan, heat 1/2 teaspoon margarine and 2 small green onions. Braise for a few minutes. Add four (4) tablespoons grated cucumber. Pepper to taste. Add 2 sprinkles Mrs. Dash and four (4) tablespoons plain yogurt. Pour over fish.

Plantation Lū'au

Donn was famous for the grand lū'au he threw at his "Plantation" in California, with Hollywood celebrities—including Bing Crosby, Vivien Leigh, Gary Cooper, and Clark Gable—as guests. The menu for Donn's feasts included salted roasted Kukui nuts ('inamona), 'opihi and limu ('opihi a me limu), dried squid with red salt (pa'akai 'ula'ula), dried aku (aku kō'ala), steamed crabs (pāpa'i māhu i'a), mullet packed in ti leaves (lāwalu 'ama'ama), kālua pig (kālua pua'a), baked sweet potatoes ('uala maola ho'omo'a), poi, chicken and lū'au in coconut milk (moa, lū'au, a ma wai niu), lomi salmon (kāmano lomi), bananas (mai'a), coconut pudding (haupia), fresh pineapple (hala kahiki), and fruit punch, along with his exotic rum concoctions.

Mahimahi a la Marama

Serves: 4 • Preparation Time: 2-1/2 hours
Complementary Dishes: Salad, Rosemary potatoes, zucchini, tomatoes
and onions sautéed with Italian seasoning.
Salt and pepper to taste, 1/2 teaspoon sugar optional.

2 pounds mahimahi – tail pieces
Olive oil for marinating
Flour for dusting
Pepper, salt, Ajinomoto,
   onion salt to taste
2 tablespoons butter
2 tablespoons olive oil
1-1/2 ounces vermouth
3 green onions – chopped
Juice of 1 lime

Marinate mahimahi in olive oil for 2 hours.
Lightly dust with flour. Sprinkle with salt,
pepper, Ajinomoto and onion salt. Fry in
half butter and olive oil. Pour into a
glass one and a half (1-1/2) ounces of
vermouth. Add chopped green onions
and the juice of one (1) lime. Toss into
pan and add vermouth. Tightly close lid
for 1 minute. Serve immediately.

Feast of the Islands

At his South Pacific Village in Waikīkī the Beach-comber put on lū'au that were first-rate and legendary. They were the first commercial lū'au presented in Hawai'i. But not just anyone could attend. One had to have a personal invitation from the Beachcomber himself. Of course, if you knew him or were staying at the Royal Hawaiian Hotel, the invites came automatically with your arrival in Honolulu.

And no one knew how to throw a party any better than Don the Beachcomber. His years of doing business in Hollywood and Chicago, along with his experiences in Italy during the war, and most of all the experience of the many lū'au he held at his Encino "Plantation" in California, had fully prepared him for the success that was to follow.

Dressed in his traditional wide-brimmed Tahitian Pandanus hat, he sported a bare chest with a necklace of wild boar tusks and a maile lei around his neck. A lava-lava covered him from the waist down. With bare feet completing the picture, the Beachcomber presented an unexpected but pleasant sight for the eyes of the many visitors to the Islands who came to his Sunday "Feast of the Islands." And most did.

Donn Beach, a.k.a. Don the Beachcomber, not only a famed restaurateur and entrepreneur, but also a pioneer in the field of tourism, was changing the face of that industry in Hawai'i. Forever.

Don's Jambalaya

Serves: 4 • Preparation Time: 2 hours
Complementary Dishes: Salad, Cornbread

1-1/2 cups shrimp (medium size)
1 medium onion – chopped
3/4 cup chopped red and green pepper
1 large clove garlic – chopped
1/2 cup chopped celery
3 tablespoons olive oil
2 tablespoons butter
1 16-ounce can stewed tomatoes
3/4 cup chopped cooked ham
1 cooked hot Italian sausage – sliced
1 cup uncooked white long grain rice
1 tablespoon olive oil
1 tablespoon butter
2 cups chicken broth
3 cloves
1 teaspoon sugar
3 dashes Worcestershire sauce
2 pinches ground nutmeg
3 tablespoons chopped parsley
4 leaves sweet basil – chopped
2 ounces very dry sherry

Sauté chopped onion, red and green pepper, garlic clove and celery in three (3) tablespoons olive oil and two (2) tablespoons butter for 15 minutes at medium heat. Add 1 sixteen (16) ounce can of stewed tomatoes. Cook for 5 minutes. Add cooked ham and Italian sausage and cook another 5 minutes. In a separate skillet, heat butter and olive oil (one tablespoon each). Pour in rice and brown slowly, stirring constantly so as not to burn. Add 2 cups chicken broth and simmer for 15 minutes. Add onion, red and green pepper mixture. Add cloves, sugar, Worcestershire sauce, ground nutmeg and stir. Add 1-1/2 cups clean, deveined pan shrimp cut into bite-size pieces. Cover and let simmer until all moisture is absorbed. Add parsley and sweet basil and at the last minute two (2) ounces very dry sherry. Stir well and let rest for about 5 minutes before serving.

Side ✳ ✳ Dishes

Don the Beachcomber (in the white hat) studying sugarcane harvesting in Jamaica.

Cook Island
Banana Loaf

Serves: 6 • Preparation Time: 2 hours
Complementary Dishes: Zest of orange mixed with butter

I cup minced dried bananas
I cup boiling water
I teaspoon baking soda
I tablespoon butter
I small cup brown sugar
I tablespoon golden syrup or honey
1/8 teaspoon pure vanilla
1/4 cup finely chopped toasted macadamia nuts
2 cups flour
I teaspoon baking powder

Into a medium mixing bowl add minced dried bananas. Pour on baking soda dissolved in a cup of boiling water. Add butter, golden syrup, sugar, salt, vanilla, basted macadamia nuts and stir for 1 minute. Fold in sifted flour and baking powder and bake in a loaf pan for 1 hour at 350 degrees.

Among The Banana Trees

While living in the Cook Islands in the 1970s, Donn Beach came upon something very unexpected while visiting the motus of Mauke and Mitiaro. Growing wild among the banana orchards, this unexpected discovery was nothing more than a problem weed to the Cook Islanders, who whacked away at the bushy pest with machetes. To the Beachcomber, the maile vines were immediately recognized as a godsend for the Hawaiian floral industry.

With the assistance of Cook Island women, the Beachcomber launched a small maile lei export enterprise, and his efforts did not go unrewarded. By the early 1980s more than five hundred maile leis were arriving at the Honolulu International Airport every week for sale to florists in Honolulu.

Although Cook Island maile has less fragrance when fresh, it is a much fuller plant than the variety growing in Hawai'i. Even today, maile grown in the Hawaiian Islands is difficult to access, and not enough of it can be picked to keep up with the demand.

Lyonnaise Potatoes

Serves: 4 • Preparation Time: 45 minutes
Complementary Dishes: A delicious accompaniment to steak dishes.
Manoa lettuce salad with Italian dressing.

4 medium-size onions
1 teaspoon sugar
2-1/2 pounds red medium
    potatoes
Freshly ground pepper
Salt, butter, parsley

In a skillet, sauté four (4) medium onions, thinly sliced, in 1/2 stick or 1/4 cup butter over medium heat, turning frequently for about 10 minutes. Add one (1) teaspoon sugar and salt to taste and cook the onions, covered for a few minutes more. In a heavy skillet, melt five (5) to six (6) tablespoons butter until it is hot, but not turning color. Add the potatoes, boiled (but still firm) and sliced, and sauté them gently, turning them as they brown. Season with salt and freshly ground pepper to taste. Add onions and toss lightly until well blended. Transfer the potatoes and onions to a serving dish and sprinkle with chopped parsley.

Cracking coconuts for a refreshing drink with two lovely wāhine.

WhiteBeans

Serves: 4 • Preparation Time: 24 hours soaking, plus 2-1/2 hours
Complementary Dishes: Light salad, French baguette

1 package northern white beans – dry
1 tablespoon salt
2 quarts water
2 quarts chicken stock
1 large onion – chopped
1/2 cup chopped bell pepper
1/2 cup chopped carrots
1/2 cup chopped celery
1 teaspoon black pepper
1 teaspoon Mrs. Dash – Red Pepper One
1 teaspoon Maggi Arome

Soak beans overnight, covered in water, salted with one (1) tablespoon salt. In the morning, rinse thoroughly. To a large pot, add beans, 2 quarts water and 2 quarts chicken stock. Bring to a boil and simmer for 1 hour, then add the rest of the ingredients. Cook until soft, approximately 1 hour. Add more chicken broth if necessary. Before serving, add 1/2 cup parsley.

Vegetable Orientale

Serves: 2 • Preparation Time: 20 minutes
Complementary Dishes: Steamed rice, Steak Genghis Kahn for Four

1/2 cup sliced celery – blanch for 1 minute
1/2 cup sliced green peppers – blanch for 1 minute
1 cup snow peas – blanch for 1 minute
1 cup sliced Maui onions
3 tablespoons olive oil
1/8 tablespoon black pepper to season
1/2 teaspoon Ajinomoto
1/4 teaspoon salt
1 teaspoon sugar
2 cups sliced Peking cabbage

Heat olive oil in a large skillet. Braise onions, peppers, peas and celery for 3 minutes, stirring to prevent burning. Stir in sliced Peking cabbage, sugar, salt, pepper and Ajinomoto. Cover and simmer for 3 minutes. Sprinkle with toasted sesame seed and chopped green onion.

Desserts

Don's
SOUFFLÉ

Serves: 4 • Preparation Time: 30 minutes
Complementary Dishes: Tahitian coffee

2 egg whites
2 egg yokes
1/2 lemon – juice only
6 tablespoons vanilla sugar
2-1/2 tablespoons flour
1/2 teaspoon butter
1 tablespoon jelly – guava or
    strawberry
1 tablespoon cream

Beat egg whites at medium speed till they form soft peaks. Add vanilla sugar and lemon juice. Beat until stiff and shiny. Add egg yokes and two and a half (2-1/2) Tablespoons flour. Put butter, jelly and cream in bottom of baking dishes. Put mixture in three (3) mountain peaks in dishes. Bake for 8 to 10 minutes at 325 degrees. Sprinkle with powdered sugar. Serve immediately.

Flaming
Fujiyama Dessert

Serves: 4 • Preparation Time: 20 minutes

> 4 tablespoons shredded coconut
> 4 scoops vanilla ice cream
> 4 teaspoons brandy

Place a bed of shredded coconut in a dessert dish. Add a cone-shaped scoop of vanilla ice cream. Sprinkle with more shredded coconut and pour brandy over it. Light the brandy, which toasts the shredded coconut for added flavor.

Papaya Royal

Serves: 2

1 medium-size ripe papaya
6 tablespoons coconut cream
2 scoops premium vanilla ice cream
1/2 ounce R.L. Seale's rum
2 dashes Angostura bitters
1/2 ounce kirschwasser
Twist of orange peel (colored part only)

Preheat oven to 400 degrees.

Cut papaya in half and scoop out seeds. Add to each half two (2) tablespoons of coconut cream. Put papaya halves in a small baking dish and bake at 400 degrees for 30 minutes.

Remove from oven and place under broiler for 3 to 4 minutes or until crust has formed.

Remove from broiler and place papaya halves in a shallow serving dish. Fill cavities with a scoop each of ice cream. Divide remaining coconut cream and pour over ice cream. Bring to table.

In a small pan, heat rum, bitters, kirschwasser and orange peel. Bring to table quickly and pour over ice cream and papaya. Use long match to set aflame.

DON the BEACHcomber
Party Guide

Don the Beachcomber made his reputation as a great host by entertaining with an extraordinary attention to detail. Food and drink were given top billing, and he made sure that everything he served was in the peak of freshness. He abhorred buffets, because he believed that food that sat for any length of time would no longer be fit to be eaten. He was especially exacting when entertaining at home. With the exception of cocktail parties, he preferred that the party be limited to a maximum of eight people, and that the food be served by course. This way, he'd be able to ensure the quality of the cuisine and the conversation.

To entertain Beachcomber style, you can choose to serve a large number of people with a selection of pūpū (see the pūpū party menu) or you might choose a sample dinner menu for an intimate party of eight or less. (If you will be serving more than four, be sure to double the recipes.) Either

way, the idea is to have *fun,* and, of course, colorful tropical drinks will always be welcome.

DÉCOR

Tropical fruits and flowers, coconuts, seashells, glass floats and rattan furniture are props that Don the Beachcomber used to set the scene for his exotic meals, and would be highly appropriate for table settings and decorating the guest bathroom. The poolside is a natural setting for a Beachcomber party, and the pool will look especially beautiful with flowers and candles floating in it. Colorful pareus, batiks and other

fabrics with tropical prints would make excellent tablecloths for the occasion.

DRESS

Don was best known for popularizing the safari look that featured short-sleeved khaki shirts with epaulets and Bermuda shorts for daywear—changing to long khaki trousers and long-sleeved safari shirts in the evening. He dressed this way because he believed that comfort is key to elegance. Certainly this look would be appropriate for a Beachcomber party, and many other comfortable and tropical options are available. These would include aloha shirts, loose-fitting caftans, mu'umu'u and pareus. Flower or shell leis will lend a festive air, and will make the guests feel welcome.

A PŪPŪ PARTY MENU

The following recipes would make a good selection of treats for a poolside party:

Green Shoyu Bean Pūpū
    Poisson Cru
    Chilled Cauliflower Salad

Chinese Hawaiian Barbecue Ribs
Tahitian Shrimps
White Sands Champagne Jubilee

DINNER PARTY MENUS

Here are a couple of menu suggestions for a dinner party:

Menu 1
Salad Supreme
Steak Genghis Khan
Steamed White Rice*
Vegetable Orientale
Flaming Dessert

Menu 2
Mixed Field Greens with Papaya
    Dressing
Mahimahi a la Marama
Lyonnaise Potatoes
Sautéed Zucchini, Onion and
    Tomatoes*
Don's Soufflé

Recipe not listed in this book.

MOVIE SUGGESTIONS

During or after dinner, a fun option would be to show a South Pacific-

themed movie. A number of entertaining titles are available in video form, including:

The White Flower	1923
South Pacific	1958
Hula	1927
Blue Hawaii	1961
Waikiki Wedding	1937
Ride the Wild Surf	1964
Hawaii Calls	1938
Goin' Coconuts	1978
Song of the Islands	1942
North Shore	1987
Ma and Pa Kettle in Waikiki	1955

RUM TASTING

For those interested in exploring the subtleties of rum, a tasting would be an excellent way to compare rum types and brands. One could assign rums of different types or countries to be brought by each guest so that a good variety could be sampled. Premium aged rums approach cognac and fine whiskey in smoothness, so snifters may be the best tasting glasses for this exercise. Be sure to provide paper for each participant for tasting notes. This is an excellent way to start interesting conversations, provided you're not too generous with the samples!

Any or all of these ideas could be incorporated into your party, but by all means don't be limited by what's written here. Your personal creative touch is all it would take to make your party special.

Don the Beachcomber and guests enjoy the lū'au fare.

The exclusive guest lists for Don the Beachcomber's grand lū'au at his Encino
"Plantation" in California included some of Hollywood's hottest stars—Bing Crosby,
Hoagy Carmichal, Alice Faye, Clark Gable, Vivien Leigh, and Gary Cooper, to name a few.

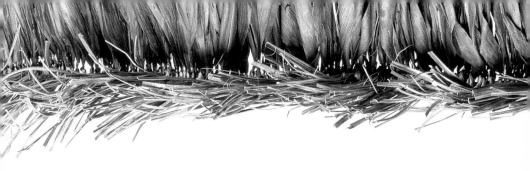

RUM GUIDE

Don the Beachcomber built his reputation by being a rum connoisseur who stocked 138 brands of rums in his restaurant. Of course, the average rum drinker wouldn't want to go through that sort of expense. The following is a rough guide that will help define the different types of rums so that, if necessary, you may substitute rums that you might already have in your collection for those called for in the recipes.

WHITE / LIGHT / SILVER

These rums are colorless, light-bodied and dry, and are used as a neutral base for cocktails and mixed drinks. Most light rums are not aged, though aged ones do exist. Some of the light rums mentioned in this book are:

> Bacardi Light
> Myers's Platinum White
> Ronrico Light

GOLDEN / ORO / AMBRÉ

This designation is used for medium-bodied, slightly sweet rums that have spent some time in oak barrels. The golden color comes from the wood,

though in some cases it is enhanced with the addition of caramel. This type of rum gives a more emphatic flavor to mixed drinks. The following are examples of this type:

> Appleton Special
> Bacardi Gold
> Hana Bay Premium Gold

DARK / BLACK

These are traditional, full-bodied rums with a strong molasses flavor that are aged in heavily charred barrels. Strongly aromatic, they are primarily designed for sipping, though they are skillfully used to add character to Don the Beachcomber's tropical drinks.

> Myers's Original Dark
> Ronrico Dark
> Lemon Hart 80 Proof
> British Navy

PREMIUM AGED / AEJO / RUM VIEUX

These well-matured rums correlate to the highly prized single malt whiskies or cognac. As rum ages, it becomes

Don the Beachcomber welcomes Anita Colby to one of his famous lūʻau.

mellower and smoother as it taps tannin, flavor and color from the oak barrel that holds it. Designed to be savored as an after-dinner drink, these rums add a touch of class.

Myers's Legend
Ron Zacapo Centenario

OVERPROOF

These generally are white rums that are bottled at 75.5 percent (151 proof) alcohol by volume. In this book, much use is made of Lemon Hart Demerara 151—which is a dark overproof rum. You might consider substituting the readily available Bacardi 151 Overproof, a gold rum.

FLAVORED AND SPICED

These are specialty rums that have been flavored with fruits or spices. Note that there are many varieties—they may not be easily substituted.

St. James Pineapple Rum
(pineapple)
Captain Morgan Parrot Bay
(clear rum with coconut)
Captain Morgan Private Stock
(spiced golden rum)

DON'S PEARL
White Rums, tropical fruit syrups, Mexican limes---every fifth drink contains a beautiful pearl.

QUEEN'S ROAD COCKTAIL
Trinidad Rum, green allspice liqueur, orange blossom honey, Angostura bitters and Acapulco limes.

DON THE BEACHCOMBER ®

In his lifetime, Don the Beachcomber invented more than ninety tropical rum drinks, including the world-famous Mai Tai. In 1939, the leaders of the rum industry acknowledged his expertise with the honorary title: "Ambassador of Rum."

I Had A Lovely Time

by John Kay
In Memory of
Don the Beachcomber

When at last my end shall come
The end of song and rhyme
Please remember this of me
I had a lovely time

I frolicked over many lands
And over many seas
And everywhere found light and cheer
And health and joy and ease

The hearts and hands of many friends
Have clasped mine as we pass
And I in turn have loved them all
And will until the last

Remember of me as I go
To whatever scene or clime
That in this world I sadly leave
I had a lovely time

About the Authors

*Arnold Bitner is married to Phoebe Beach. Arnold saw the possibilities
of the Don the Beachcomber story when he became aware of the
material within the extensive collection of memorabilia
Donn Beach left to Phoebe. Arnold was fascinated with
Donn's life and the innovations Donn brought to the tourism industry,
both in Hawai'i, and to other nations of the Pacific Rim. It wasn't long
before Arnold set about putting the Beachcomber's story to paper.
He was the driving force behind the project, and this book is the result.*

*Phoebe Beach is Don the Beachcomber's widow. Phoebe longed to have
Donn's story told, and Arnold helped to make her dream come true.
Phoebe worked with Arnold in compiling the details for the drink and
food recipes, and she edited the final manuscript.*

*Arnold and Phoebe live in Hawai'i.
Visit their website at www.hawaiibeachcomber.com*